W9-BKG-905

Shakespeare
Well-Versed

KING HENRY V
MACBETH
OTHELLO
HENRY VI Reel 12
HAMLET
KING LEAR
THE TEMPEST
TWELFTH NIGHT
ROMEO & JULIET
PERICLES
NUTZ

Shakespeare *Well-Versed*

A Rhyming Guide to All His Plays

PG

James Muirden

illustrations by
David Eccles

Walker & Company
New York

First published in the United States of America in 2004
by Walker Publishing Company, Inc.;
published simultaneously in Great Britain by
Constable & Robinson Ltd as *Shakespeare in a Nutshell.*

For information about permission to reproduce selections from this book, write to Permissions, Walker & Company, 104 Fifth Avenue, New York, New York 10011.

Library of Congress Cataloging-in-Publication Data
available upon request
ISBN 0-8027-1441-2

Visit Walker & Company's Web site at
www.walkerbooks.com

Printed in the United States of America

2 4 6 8 10 9 7 5 3 1

To my tutors at St. Luke's, Exeter

Edwyn Crowle
Brian Merrick
Mike Russell

With affectionate thanks

1st
EPISODE
OF THE
History
Plays
Richard II
INK

Introduction

School turned me right off Shakespeare. Twenty years later, as a 'mature' student taking a teaching degree in English, I met him again. As Mark Twain remarked of his parents, it was amazing how much more sensible he had become by the time I had grown up.

A little while ago, I noticed an advertisement for a television programme that would try to make *Romeo and Juliet* more 'accessible' to young people. Various pre-programme activities were suggested, the last and least being to try to read a scene or two of the actual play — implying that the text itself is a monster to be attacked with a long-handled implement.

The text certainly is one of the hurdles. Shakespeare's language is unfamiliar both in word-meaning and in sentence construction. Furthermore, his plays were written for actors who, by our standards, did not 'act' at all — they declaimed rather than 'performed'. We habitually speak of going to the theatre to 'see' a play, but the Tudors and Stuarts went to the playhouse to *hear* a play. The Prologue to *Henry V* invites the audience 'Gently to hear, kindly to judge', and Hippolyta, when Bottom and his thespians entertain the newly-weds at the end of *A Midsummer Night's Dream*, says 'This is the silliest stuff that ever I heard'. It is the modern actor's function to transmit the essential clues contained in the text; to Tudor audiences this may have been less necessary.

Second, Shakespeare's audiences probably went to the theatre well-primed with pre-performance information. Most of his plots were re-hashes of existing stories, so that even if the play was new to them, the characters and situation may well have been familiar. His historical saga — that Himalayan range extending across eight plays, from Richard II to Richard III — presented the saints and villains of the familiar past. So he could just launch into the action, and the viewers (hearers!) would know who most of them were without being told. Modern audiences need more help.

So I hope that this book will prove to be a convenient and enjoyable introduction to Shakespeare's plays. I hope, too, that by giving the rarely performed works as much prominence as the heavyweights, it may encourage you to keep an eye out for their rare staging, or borrow a video — or even try *reading* them as short stories! Much wonderful writing is buried in the unfamiliar plays. Why not dust off that anthology and let him speak to you directly?

Constable's Carol O'Brien suggested that I tackle this project, and I am grateful for her encouragement and constructive criticism. As always, my wife Helen has been a tower of strength, and my son Dan has offered some helpful actors' perspectives. The 'decorations' received from David Eccles in response to my batches of rough drafts have been a constant stimulus to keep him supplied with more.

JAMES MUIRDEN

To the Onlie Begetter

As gold prospectors, by a flowing streame,
Dredge uppe great quantities of useless sand
Before they're greeted by the faintest gleame
Of precious mettal in the stuff they've pann'd
So did you, fair Begetter, scan my pages
For signs of talent in the dross I'd written,
Till, after wee had been in touch for ages,
You chose A RHYMING HISTORY of BRITAIN.
Enhanc'd once more by David's decoration,
Our greatest Poet here appeares in rhyme;
So please accept this humble dedication
From these your servants, now & for alle time;
And thank you for your bountiful consent
To give us both an extra Two Percent.

Jas. Muirden
& David Eccles

The Plays

Notes

The approximate dates of composition are shown. A question mark indicates an uncertainty of more than a year or two.

The line references given in the text are to the Arden edition.

All's Well That Ends Well

Is Helena a little schemer,
Or does her captive heart redeem her?
If Oscar Wilde's right to say
That truth is never found half-way,
She stands at one of these extremes;
And modern estimation seems
To take the less approving view
Of what this girl sets out to do.
The play's seen as a kind of primer
On how to be a social climber
And trick your way into the bed
Of someone far above your head.
I wonder, though, if this is what
Shakespeare intended? Here's the plot.

*

Young Bertram's father's dead and gone,
So he's now Count of Rousillon, [I, i]
And, newly titled, has to go
To see the King, who's feeling low —

There's something wrong with his inside,
And though Top Specialists have tried
To minister to his attacks,
He obviously thinks they're quacks.
Now Helen (Helena is sweeter,
But doesn't always suit the metre),
The orphan of a famed physician,
Was kindly given a position
In Bertram's home. The old Countess
Is like a mother; nevertheless,
Helen is smitten by her son!
This is the prelude to Scene 1,
In which she muses on how far
She dwells below his shining
  star:
But though he's way above her sphere,
Might not their earthly hearts cohere?†
She therefore packs and goes post-
  haste
To give the ailing King a taste

Of Father's
  noxious prophylactic —
As she admits to us, a tactic
That's less inspired by his plight
Than keeping Bertram in her sight.

[I, iii]

*

† *Helena*. Our remedies oft in ourselves do lie,
Which we ascribe to heaven. [I, i, 212]

She tells the monarch, when they meet:
'You'll soon be up and on your feet; [II, i]
And as a token of your thanks
I'll choose a husband from your ranks.'
The bargain made — surprise, surprise!
The King is cured before our eyes!
The nervous nobles congregate: [II, iii]
Helen pretends to cogitate,
Then collars Bertram, who, nonplussed,
Does not conceal his disgust.
Up to this point, I must admit,
I think he's got the worst of it —
Nobody fancies being chased
By someone foreign to their taste.

But now begin a string of follies
Encouraged by his friend Parolles
(Whose escapades, I ought to say,
Take up a good part of the play).
He leaves her with her maidenhead, [II, v]
And goes off to the wars instead,
Writing a pretty nasty letter
That hints he's anxious to forget her: [III, ii]
'You will not be my wife, until

You've got my ring (you never will),
And have a baby on the way
Conforming to my DNA.
P.S. Until you pack and go,
I won't return. A bientôt.'

*

Of course, these most unlikely things
Are what *will* happen! Bertram's flings
In Florence lead him to Diana,
A virtuous girl in mind and manner,
Whose charms so far she has denied;
Meanwhile poor Helen's mortified
To hear her husband won't come back,
And leaves for the convent of St Jacques. [III, v]
By chance, she bumps into no other
Than chaste Diana and her mother,
Who, like most others in the street,
Find it quite hard to make ends meet.
The three of them draw up a charter [III, vii]
By which Bertram's inamorata
Will, for a certain sum, agree
By night (so that he cannot see),
To let him share her waiting bed —

Though really Helen's there instead.
The ring's pulled off — and lots more too,
Before her hoodwinked husband's through.

*

Do I need to describe the rest?
The happy outcome you'll have guessed!
Bertram's exposed before the King [V, iii]
For giving up his precious ring
To win Diana (as he thought —
For everything comes out in court);
And, since she's pregnant with his child,
Helen and he are reconciled.

At several points, it seems to me,
Abstraction and reality
Conflict within this 'problem play' —
But don't let *that* keep you away!

Antony and Cleopatra

This *Alexandrine* format, which has six iambic feet
(Each 'foot' contains two stresses, and gives the line its beat,
While 'iambic' means the emphasis is on the second stress),
Is rarely used for poems, since it's rather colourless.
However, this late tragedy is somewhat grey in parts —
And Alexandria, you see, is where the story starts.

The Bard wrote other plays about tall men who were
brought down
By pride (Coriolanus), or were tempted by the crown
(Macbeth of course), or jealousy (which undermined
Othello),
While lack of judgement made King Lear a most unstable
fellow.
Mark Antony, however, meets a different kind of fate:
His love for Egypt's Queen exceeds his duty to the State.

For Love and Duty to conflict, has furnished many a tale;
But never, we are meant to think, on such a massive scale
As when Mark Antony was stunned by Cleopatra's charms —
A lady who'd already lain in
Julius Caesar's arms,
And gave birth to Caesarion
in 47 BC
(The first in her extensive
single-parent family).

The mordant Enobarbus,
whose asides will ridicule
Mark Antony's enslavement,
thinks him an utter fool:
Yet he shows his admiration, in describing how he saw
The wavelets, stroked to madness by each rower's
rhythmic oar,
Surge after Cleopatra's barge, and tumble in her wake —
A pretty forceful image of the impact she could make. [II, ii, 190]

She was brought to him by water, for a cross-examination
To see what grounds, if any, were behind the allegation
That she'd secretly colluded with Rome's enemies abroad —
And she turned out so collusive that he simply stayed
on board.

Their passion's overwhelming: she wants him more and more,
And Antony sees much more sense in making Love,
not War! [I, i]

Octavius Caesar calls him home. Though carrying most weight,
He, Antony, and Lepidus form a triumvirate
(The Roman nation is so large, it's cut up into parts,
Each ruling his own share of it — and so dissension starts).
Our hero's lately widowed, so he marries Caesar's
sister — [II, ii]
Then back to Cleopatra's place, to say how much
he's missed her. [III, vii]

Octavius fights Lepidus — that's one less triumvar.
Meanwhile, in Alexandria, the lovers go too far.
The lands controlled by Antony are given to their brood, [III, vi]
And Cleopatra's crowned as Isis. This ineptitude

Is naturally headline news: Octavius is cross,
And launches all his warships, to show the pair who's boss.

At Actium, near Corfu, in the blue Ionian Sea,
Queen Cleopatra's sixty galleys turn around and flee.
Mark Antony's to go with her — Enobarbus sees their flight
And says (Act 3, Scene 10): 'Mine eyes did sicken at
the sight.' [III, x, 17]
Now back in Egypt, Antony has got his suitcase packed:
When teams are relegated, it's the manager that's sacked.

But though they're at rock bottom, instead of arguing
(The usual course), we witness an unprecedented thing.
She weeps and begs forgiveness for reducing him to this,
But he tells her it was worth it, and she lets him have
a kiss.
Inspired, he tells Octavius he'll come and take him on —
Which is proof to Enobarbus that the fellow's wits
are gone. [III, xiii]

The 'lion's whelp' (Octavius) is not exactly keen
On single-handed combat, so he messages the Queen
To leave her dotty consort, and come to him instead.
She (fine dissembler!) says she will; and Antony, misled,
Accuses her, engendering a melting protestation.
'Now he'll outstare the lightning' — Enobarbus's
quotation! [III, xiii, 195]

Octavius sails to Egypt, and Act 4 sees lots of fighting —
It runs to fifteen scenes, so you can tell it's most exciting.
On land, the battle's Antony's; but we have seen before
That his lady's useless navy has no appetite for war.
Its surrender makes him think that she has turned
to Rome instead —
So to make him feel sorry, she claims that she is dead. [IV, xii]

Things now get rather out of hand: Mark Antony's remorse
Leaves him no option but to take the Noble
Roman course. [IV, xiv]
But he bungles it, and learns that Cleopatra
was pretending,
So he's carted off for what should be a
scintillating ending.
She's immured aloft for safety,
and somewhat disinclined
To come down; so he's hauled
up with a bit of rope they find. [IV, xv]

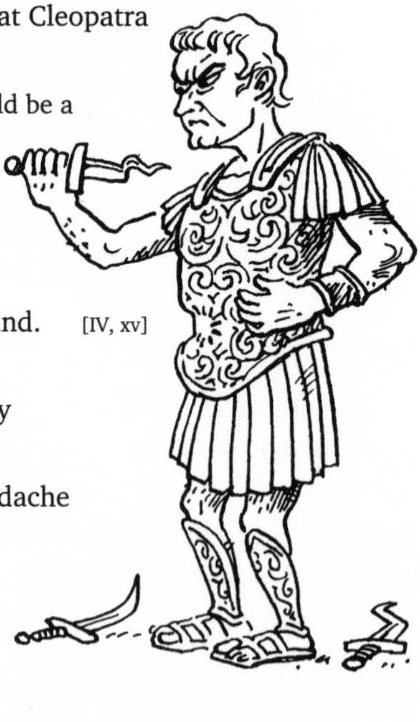

Yanking him up her multi-storey
monument has been,
For many stage directors, a headache
of a scene.

To have your hero dangle in a basket in mid-air,
And then expire with dignity, needs more than
normal care.
There's another hurdle also — a poetic one this time . . .
The asp, *vipera aspis*, a snake with no known rhyme.

The most accomplished actress can find it
quite a test
To tear her clothes and clutch a writhing
serpent to her breast
And deliver devastating stuff in praise
of Antony,
Which epitaphs them both, and seals their
immortality. [V, ii]
But Plutarch, Shakespeare's source, insists
that this is what she did:
So be careful with a box of figs, before you
lift the lid!

As You Like It

As You Like It isn't 'real' —
But the pastoral ideal
(Deeply rooted in our senses)
Speaks to modern audiences.
Sell your house and go abroad . . .
Buy somewhere you can afford . . .
What provides the motivation?
Lower levels of taxation?
Legacy? Retirement?
In this play it's *Banishment*!

*

Duke Frederick has usurped his brother
On some trumped-up charge or other.
The outlawed Duke, it's widely said,
Quite enjoys his forest bed:

His daughter (sprightly Rosalind)
Had been allowed to stay behind
When Father went into the wild,
With cousin Celia, Frederick's child. [I, ii]
But Shakespeare has a second plot
(A method he employs a lot)
Following a similar line,
With which the first will intertwine . . .
Orlando's rightful claim to lands
Firmly in his brother's hands
Has been demeaningly denied
Ever since their father died. [I, i]
To take his mind off his position
He puts in for a competition
To see if anyone can throw
The Duke's own champion; and so
He's spied by Rosalind, whose heart [I, ii]
(Like his) is hit by Cupid's
dart —

. . .

Once their glances have cohered,
Love's ordained course must be steered.
Now the wrestling has begun . . .
Incredible! Orlando's won!
Not much time for celebration —
He gathers, to his consternation,
That Brother (and the Duke) intend [II, iii]
To bring him to a sticky end . . .
In fact, the Duke's in such a stew
That Rosalind's told to clear off too!
Celia, empathetic twin,
Goes off with her; and so begin
These maidens' exploits — in disguise
That fools the other actors' eyes

But not our own (I ought to mention
This old theatrical convention). [I, iii]
Rosalind's the 'male lead',
Known to all as Ganymede,
Celia is Aliena
(His sister); while their entertainer
Touchstone (motley Fool) makes three.
To Arden's forest they all flee,
Orlando making his own way —
They'll meet up later in the play.

*

Shakespeare's different wild spots
Serve many functions in his plots;
But Arden's in a natural state
Where simplest feelings operate.
Problems happen, even so,
As Silvius and Phebe show . . .
The disproportionate disdain
With which proud Phebe treats her swain
(For both are humble folk indeed)
Ignites the heart of Ganymede,
Who tells her she could do far worse, [III, v]
Her passion turning prose to verse —
Always a sign of earnestness.
So now we have a proper mess:
When Phebe sees this handsome youth
Her swain seems even more uncouth . . .

This Ganymede's the man for her!
Yet Silvius does not demur
From carrying her ardent letter:
A subtler fellow would know better,
But he's the picture of devotion,
A happy slave to his emotion.
Meanwhile, messages appear,
Showing that Orlando's near . . .
Each a passionate entreaty
To Rosalind. These
    sweet graffiti
Should surely make her
    start confessing
To her expedient cross-dressing
When they meet, as they shortly will? [IV, i]
But she must stay in rôle until,
In due course, a transcendent art
Will liberate her from her part!

So what can this transvestite do,
Since no man may another woo?
'Now look,' she says, 'if you'd be free [V, iv]
Of your disease, make love to me.†
I'll play your girl, be most unkind,
And cure you of Rosalind.'
(In *Twelfth Night* there's more exploitation
Of comic gender permutation.)
Harsh allocation overtakes
My pen . . . I haven't mentioned Jaques,
Who tells us 'All the world's a stage,' [II, vii]
Or how Orlando's brother's rage
Evaporates, and he is smitten [V, ii]
By Celia: but what I've written
Will be enough, I hope, to show
That if it's playing, you should go!

---

† In case your prudent soul dissents,
I mean in the old-fashioned sense. [II, vii, 139]

The Comedy of Errors

The *Comedy of Errors*
Is the shortest of the lot:
But although it holds no terrors
Through complexity of plot,
You must keep your concentration
From the first Act to the last,
Or the comic situation
Won't make sense before it's passed.
It depends for its success
On no one knowing who is who —
But to understand the mess
It's most important that *you* do!

*

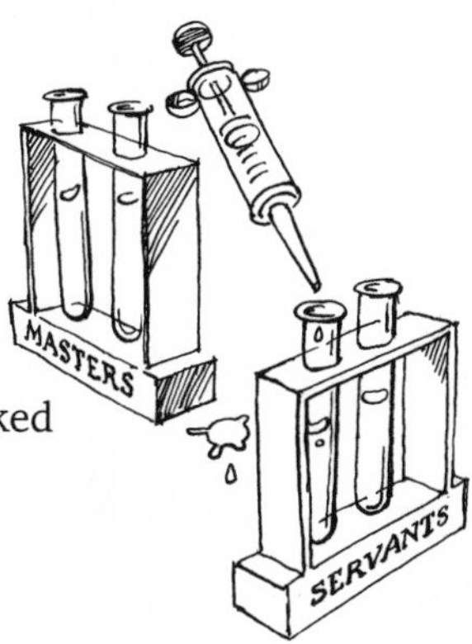

A casting difficulty starts
Before the work begins:
To play the major male parts
Requires *two* sets of twins!
Identical (as you'd expect),
They've never seen each other
Since their ill-fated ship was wrecked
And sundered every brother.
Two masters (called Antipholus),
Two servants (Dromio),
Who meet one day at Ephesus;
Here's what you need to know . . .

*

The new-born Dromios were bought
To serve each infant master;
But this arrangement was cut short
When all met with disaster.

Their parents, sailing off to start
A better life anew,
Noticed the boat had come apart,
And no sign of the crew.

With most remarkable *sang-froid*,
They found the time to lash
Each pair of infants on a spar —
Then jumped in with a splash.

*

These helpless forms (master and slave),
Securely bound together,
Reached different coasts, once wind and wave
Gave way to better weather.
Now many years have passed away . . .
One master's settled down
In Ephesus; where, on this day
His father comes to town.
This patient man still
hopes for news
About his sons or wife;

But since he comes from Syracuse,
He's forfeited his life.

*

His testimony at the start, [I, i]
Which tells what went before,
Should reconcile the hardest heart:
But the Ephesian Law,
Which seems to us extremely tough,
Dooms death, if he can't pay
(A thousand marks will be enough)
By five o'clock that day.
His second son arrives as well, [I, ii]
Plus slave, to cause confusion;
While nearby, in a cloistered cell,
Their mother's in seclusion!

*

This set-up, it's not hard to see,
Offers substantial scope
For dire misidentity —
Which was the playwright's hope.

Each slave, of course, has to endure
Many a painful whipping
From furious masters who are sure
Their loyalty is slipping;
The married brother's wife berates
His somewhat puzzled twin,
But once her wrathfulness abates
She smiles and lets him in . . . [II, ii]

*

All this is comedy, it seems:
And yet, behind the fun
There lurk some fundamental themes
Affecting everyone.
The Dromios have no defence
From blows, although we laugh:
The wandering brother has a sense
Of being just one half . . .
(Until the exposé begins, [V, i]
It's possible to see
A single actor play both twins —
But don't tell Equity!)

Coriolanus

Proudly is Caius Marcius lauded home!
His wife Virgilia leaves off her knitting [I, iii]
And joins her mother-in-law, with all of Rome,
To greet his triumph in a way that's fitting.

He's garlanded, and everyone's excited:
'That match with Corioli† was some game —
A great away win! We'd all be delighted
If you took *Coriolanus* as your name!'

But is he pleased at being adulated?
He's not, for when he sat on Mother's knee
In civic Duty was he inculcated —
Superfluous praise corrupts Integrity!

† A city of the Volscians, who dwelt
Just south of Rome, and made their presence felt.

This play raises the issue of PR.
Proud Marcius lacks the politician's guile:
He cannot word thoughts other than they are,
Or kiss strange babies with a happy smile . . .

But, since his victory has marked him down
For Consulship, he is by custom bidden
To show the fans the scars beneath his gown
(Though certain parts are, naturally, hidden). [II, i]

Now does this proud man's scornfulness show
through
The humble robe that cloaks his cuts
and gashes —
For, even though they plead to have a view,
He won't expose himself,
even in flashes. [II, iii]

Two Tribunes, Brutus and Sicinius, plan
To work on the Plebeians' discontent [II, i]
(Tribunes are voices for the Common Man —
Not that *they* get much say in government).

Knowing that Marcius's fuse is very short,
They say the people are antagonistic
And blame him for corruption — a report
That makes imperious Marcius go ballistic.

His tongue becomes his sword: you ought
to read
The molten waves that surge across the page! [III, i]
The Tribunes, and the common folk they lead,
Are vaporised in his patrician rage.

'Give power to *them*, and Rome won't last a week!
This city needs top-down administration!'
'That's treason!' shrieks Sicinius. 'What a cheek!
What is a city but its population?'†

The noise makes Mother think she ought to come
And sort things out. Volumnia's her name.
She's kept young Marcius well under her thumb —
And tells him, frankly, he's the one to blame.

† An aphorism for Democracy:
But not in Rome in 480 BC.

She says: 'You've got your image in a state! [III, ii]
Tell them you're sorry.' 'Sorry?' he replies.
'Perjure myself for that conglomerate?'
So she's left no alternative, and cries.

It does the trick: he makes a resolution
To keep his temper: but the people shout
(Urged by the Tribunes) for his execution.
'I've had enough!' he roars. 'I'm clearing out!' [IV, i]

He joins Aufidius, Rome's greatest foe, [IV, iv]
Whose Volscians are ready to attack.
Marcius is keen to get in on the show . . .
He got the boot — but Rome will get the sack!

His family now turn up in his tent, [V, iii]
And grovel at his feet. Their urgent pleas
Move him: 'Okay, we'll reach some settlement.'
(By this time all of them are on their knees.)

Aufidius's stock has fallen low
Since Marcius is far more charismatic.
This sell-out means the Roman has to go!
His liquidation's suitably dramatic ...

Cymbeline

This *should* have been a box-office success!
It's got the makings: a besieged Princess;
A subtle Villain and a fiendish Queen;
A banished lover and a Bedroom Scene;
Cross-dressing; princes taken from their bed;
A death-like drug; a man who's lost his head —
All set against the tramp of warlike feet
Brought over by Augustus Caesar's fleet.
Enough here, you would think, to make a hit!
But what's the genre? How to market it?

*

The play commences with an Explanation [I, i]
(A common ruse): some lost friend or relation
Is being told of who did what and when . . .
A way of giving us the *mise en scène*.
The set-up's briefly this. King Cymbeline
Married a second wife, a widowed Queen
Who's most unsavoury. Her oafish offspring
(Named Cloten), and the daughter of the King
(The Princess Imogen) were marked to wed;
But Imogen chose Posthumus instead.
Since Posthumus betrays no royal strain†

---

† However, with so many in disguise,
It's possible we're in for a surprise!

(An orphan brought up in the King's domain),
This nuptial has caused a royal fuss,
And banishment is served on Posthumus!

*

He's packed his things, and is about to go
To Italy, leaving Pisanio,
His faithful servant — who, it turns out later,
Is an astonishing facilitator.
The newly-weds, before their sundering,
Exchange with vows a bracelet and a ring
That will not leave their person, come what may
(Ah-ha, we think, so it's *that* sort of play —
Before *The Merchant* and *All's Well* have ended,
Rings have left fingers sooner than intended!).
All Imogen can do is moon and weep,
And do her best to catch up on her sleep,
Since clumsy Cloten's prompted
by his mother
To win her favour one way or
another . . .
The tactic that this optimist employs
Is to awake her with
melodious noise [II, iii]

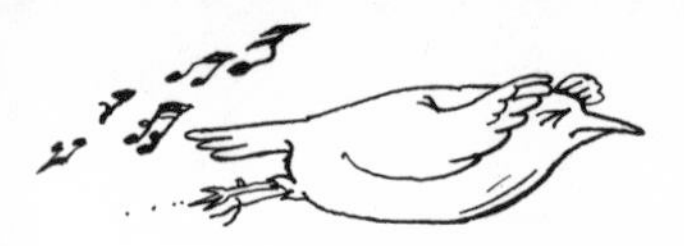

(*Hark, hark, the lark,* etc.), which, to me,
Suggests a lack of perspicacity.
Meanwhile, in Rome, a most accomplished rake,
Iachimo, tells Posthumus he'll make
A bet: 'Ten thousand ducats to your ring she'll fall
To my persuasion — winner taking all!' [I, iv]
Poor Posthumus is trapped. Should he refuse,
He's saying, in effect, he thinks he'll lose . . .
He'll show that slug how dearest Imogen
Will deal with swaggering Italian men!

Uh-huh — he's pledged the ring, so now we know
There'll be a fair amount of to-and-fro
Before *that's* once more safely on his hand!
Iachimo has sped by sea and land
(Well, obviously) . . . and after her rebuff — [I, vi]
At which point he pretends it was a bluff
To prove her honesty — he springs Plan B.
He's got a trunk of treasure: could she see

Her way to letting it stay in her room
For safety? Kindness seals her doom,
For, as I'm sure you have already guessed,
Iachimo's concealed in the chest!
Shattered by Cloten's early-morning waking,
She snoozes on while Iachimo is taking
The bracelet from her dream-entangled arms
And ogling her undefended charms. [II, ii]
Back in the box, and back to Rome, to tell
(And prove by token) that she served him well . . . [II, iv]

Imogen's unaware of his deceit,
And heads for Milford Haven, where she'll meet
(As she's led to suppose) her Posthumus —
Who's now, of course, convinced she's devious!
The plot becomes increasingly confused . . .
King Cymbeline's consistently refused

Rome's claim of tribute, so, to make him pay,
He hears a Red Reminder's on the way, [III, v]
To be delivered by a far from token force
That's swept up Imogen (disguised, of course)
Plus Iachimo and Posthumus as well.†
It would, I fear, take far too long to tell
How Imogen was cared for by her brothers [III, vi]
(Unknown to her, she likewise to the others!),
Stolen as babies and brought up in the wild
By banished Belarius, both thinking they're *his* child;
How she was aided by Pisanio, who
Her jealous spouse had told to run her through; [III, iii]
How Cloten, wearing Posthumus's togs,
Chased after her through rough terrain and bogs,
Intending to possess her in his gear
(Some serious disorder there, I fear);
How, side-tracked by a sudden
altercation,
The fellow underwent decapitation
Before he had accomplished
his desire;
How Imogen, confused by
his attire,
Supposed his corpse her
husband's own, and said:
'Oh Posthumus, alas,
where is thy head?' [IV, ii, 320]

† The microscopic chance that this should be
Is not exceptional in Comedy.

(A line, I must admit, that made me blench,
Even when spoken by Dame Judi Dench).
To say more would not help the cause one jot:
It really is a quite fantastic plot —
Act 5 Scene 5, a mass of explanations,
Has more than *twenty* different revelations.
I may, perhaps, have run it down a bit —
But I can't see it ever being a hit!

Hamlet, Prince of Denmark

Prince Hamlet's suffering from stress. [I, ii]
The reason isn't hard to guess:
Four weeks after his father died
A second marriage knot was tied
To join his freshly widowed mother
With Claudius, her husband's brother.
At Elsinore, by Denmark Sound,
The dead king's spirit wanders round,
Upsetting sentries at their post,
So they've complained about the ghost

To sceptical Horatio,
Who sees it, and lets Hamlet know.
The phantom warns his gob-smacked son:
'Your uncle is the guilty one. [I, v]
During my after-dinner snooze,
(Occasioned by excess of booze)
He seized his chance to sneak up near
And pour some poison in my ear.
Now stop your dithering about,
And go and sort the fellow out.'

*

Well, all Prince Hamlet has to do
Is knife his uncle in Act Two . . .
But audiences wouldn't pay
Unless it was a five-act play,
So Shakespeare has this thoughtful youth
Soliloquise on Cause and Truth,
Revenge, the Afterlife, etc.,
And, ultimately, his *raison d'être*.
Since Hamlet's never going to find
The answers in his tortured mind
(And since whatever can, goes wrong)
This famous play's extremely long.

*

Enter Ophelia, a part
To challenge any player's art.
Since Elsinore seems rather short

Of lusty stuff of either sort,
We're not surprised when she lets slip
There's some sort of relationship —
Polonius,† her father, senses
A weakening of her defences,
And urges her to cross
her legs

No matter how hard Hamlet begs. [I, iii]
The King and Queen ponder his theory
That Love has made the lad world-weary; [II, ii]
And, with Ophelia as bait,
The men conceal themselves and wait,
To judge of Hamlet's true desire. [III, i]
But he has heard the group conspire,
And tells the wretched girl that she
Should go into a nunnery,
Which strikes them all as somewhat strange . . .

---

† Polonius's precept to his son
(Neither a borrower nor a lender be)
If followed nowadays by everyone
Would undermine the whole economy. [I, iii 75]

The King thinks Hamlet needs a change:
The kröner's strong against the pound,
So he's to take a trip around
The sights of England, where he'll be
With others just as mad as he!

Poor Hamlet's in increasing doubt
If he can sort his tangle out
(The nature of the lad's disease
Has spawned a shelf of PhDs).
What if the ghost that met his eyes
Was just a devil in disguise,
And Uncle had been, all the time,
Quite innocent of any crime?
Then, if he knocks him off, he'll be
In hell's fire for eternity!

While he's debating right and wrong
A troupe of Players comes along;
And suddenly he sees a way
Of finding Truth within a Play.
He gets them to enact, in mime
(With Uncle watching all the time)
A king within his orchard snoring,
A villain drawing near, and pouring
Some noxious stuff into his head . . .
The king wakes up, and finds he's dead!
His uncle's guilt erupts in rage [III, ii]
When seeing this performed on stage.
The wind's set fair, the tide is in;
His nephew's journey must begin;
Though if things happen as they should
The trip won't do the Prince much good,
Since Rosencrantz and Guildenstern
(Two old school-friends) are told they'll earn
A more than generous reward
If he should vanish overboard!

*

Before he goes to pack his chest
He finds his Mother half-undressed, [III, iv]
Not knowing it's another snare —
Polonius is planted there
To overhear their private talk,
But gives out an impulsive squawk,

So Hamlet runs the fellow through.
All this domestic hullabaloo
Brings Mother to the verge of tears,
At which point Father's ghost appears
And says: 'I've had enough of waiting
While you go on procrastinating!'
The Prince, who cannot but agree,
Gets all his stuff, and puts to sea.

*

Ophelia's big scene comes next [IV, v]
It's so good you should read the text —

She's lost her wits, which is a pity,
And sings a rather risqué ditty.
So, what with one thing and another,
Laertes, her adoring brother
Shares Claudius's jaundiced view
Of what the place is coming to
With Hamlet there. The two debate [IV, vii]
How they can best annihilate
Their common foe, and make it seem
An accident! This is their scheme . . .
The lads will duel in the hall,
Before the eyes of one and all,
Laertes taking care to dip
His foil's specially sharpened tip
Into some stuff, before the bout,
That ought to sort Prince Hamlet out.

However, if he should avoid
The vegetable alkaloid
They'll offer him, to praise his play,
A nice full-bodied Cabernet,
Whose fruity, tannic depths will mask
More poison to complete the task.

*

We're getting on! It's now Act Five:
Our hero has escaped alive
From his exciting package trip,
And given everyone the slip.
Now, landed on home ground once more, [V, i]
He wanders back to Elsinore,
And sees a grave (so now we're at
'Alas poor Yorick,' and all that).
Ophelia has passed away;
Hamlet is frantic with dismay,
And then (a tricky bit to stage)
He and Laertes, in a rage,
Embark upon a graveside fight,
Fall in, and disappear from sight.

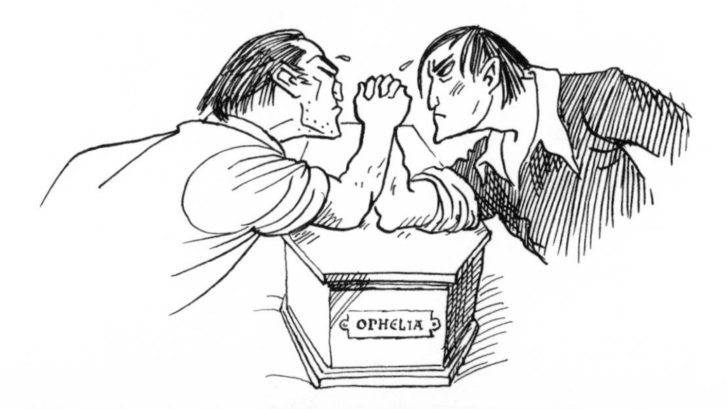

And now, at last, the duel scene,
Performed before the King and Queen; [V, ii]

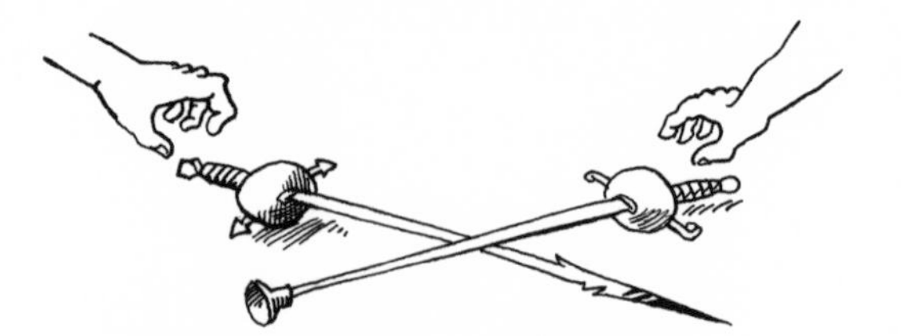

Although, as often is the way,
The best-laid plans can go astray.
Laertes gives his foe a nick
Between the bouts (a dirty trick,
Though Hamlet takes such ages dying
We wonder if he's really trying);
But then his mother cocks it up
By drinking from the poisoned cup,
While Hamlet, typically confused,
Picks up the foil Laertes used.
So now his rival's had his lot,
And gives away the devious plot,
Which makes our princely hero think
King Claudius deserves a drink,
And gets him to consume the rest —
Wine that has 'breathed' is always best . . .
And having reached the end, I see
I've missed 'To be or not to be'. [III, i, 56]

Julius Caesar

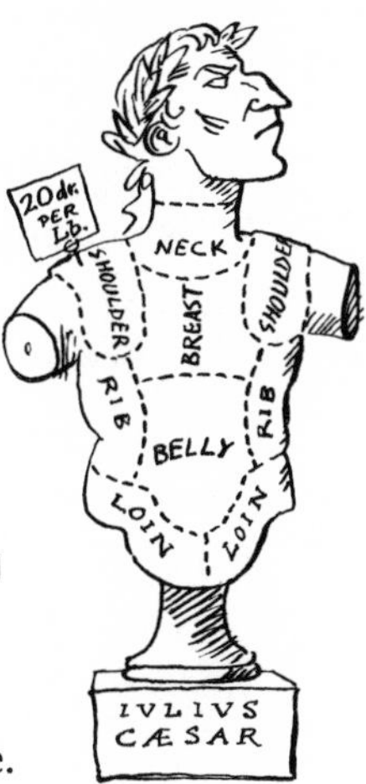

'Let's carve him as a dish fit for the
gods.' [II, i, 173)]
This play has a contemporary theme:
A group of politicians are at odds
With Caesar's plan to start a new regime.

Rome liked to reach decisions through debate:
Its government must lead, and not be led!
No ruling family, no potentate —
Elected Consuls ran the place instead.

It's marvellous, in retrospect, to think
How this outlasted plotting and sedition
Till Julius Caesar brought them to the brink
By wanting to fulfil his own ambition

To be crowned *Emperor*! This is the threat.
The plotters are extremely businesslike:
Caesar's the only one they're out to get —
His blood alone in this pre-emptive strike. [II, ii]

Here, walking in his orchard, very late, [II, i]
Is Marcus Brutus, noble Roman, who
Is marked for Caesar's place. We're told the date —
The fifteenth day of March.[†] Is this a clue?

The weather forecast got it wrong again:
A thunderstorm, graves yielding up their dead,
Disorientated lions, blazing men . . .
You'd think he ought to be tucked up in bed!

Enter Conspirators, cloak-and-dagger stuff:
Cassius, Casca, Decius and Cinna,
Metellus and Trebonius . . . that's enough.
Brutus is game — they're sure they've backed
the winner.

Mark Antony, they know, wants Caesar crowned.
He's dangerous: they ought to fix him too!
Brutus says 'No' — he'll talk the fellow round.
That's Error 1 — we'll soon see Error 2 . . .

---

† The famous Ides of March, as you'll have guessed!
Some months the 15th — the 13th for the rest.

The name of 'Brutus' does not serve him well:
Reason, not Force, is his Imperator.
His cause is politic, not personal
('Though I love Caesar, yet I love Rome more'). [III, ii, 22]

Now enter Julius in his nightgown, yawning. [II, ii]
His wife's been screaming; he's hardly slept a wink.
Calphurnia's dream — is it a Dire Warning?
His statue spouting blood! It makes you think . . .

His escort Decius discovers with dismay
He's going to stay at home. They're up the spout!
Confound Calphurnia! What can he say
To Julius, to get him to go out?

Got it! The bleeding statue, he explains,
Isn't a Portent, but a Celebration.
'You are our heart, your blood runs in our veins . . .
From you all Romans draw their inspiration!'

And Julius falls for it! 'So *that's* my fate!'
He laughs. 'Poor wife, how foolish you have been!
Bring me my gown! By Jove, it's after eight!'
(I don't need to describe the Murder Scene.) [III, i]

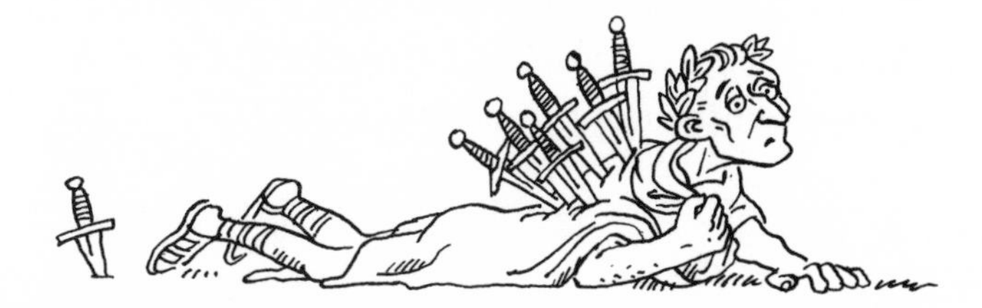

Mark Antony, of course, is most upset
At finding that his chief has been done in.
He vows to be revenged — but not just yet . . .
He needs some backing if he's going to win.

And so he shakes the butchers by the hand,
And says a friendly word or two to each,
And asks: 'I wonder if you'd kindly let me stand
Before the crowd, and make a little speech?'

Brutus says 'Fine', but Cassius is dismayed:
'You fool, you've done it now! You haven't reckoned
On how the sheep-like *hoi polloi* are swayed.
Why have you let Mark Antony speak *second*?'

Off to the Forum! Brutus talks in prose, [III, ii]
In balanced clauses; makes his point, and stops.
Mark Antony (*Friends, Romans*) strikes a pose,
Pours out pentameters, and uses props.

'If you have tears, prepare to shed them now.' [III, ii, 169]
(You'll hear a lot of quotes before he's ended.)
'Caesar's best gown — just thrown down anyhow!
Look at these holes! They might have got it mended!'

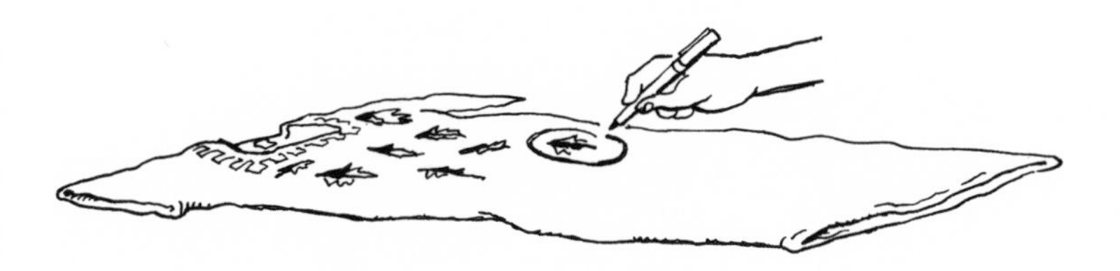

And then, after well-judged prevarication,
Comes Caesar's Will. That really gets them going!
Each man gets half a Euro[†] — jubilation!
Now Brutus sees the way the wind is blowing.

Octavius Caesar is Julius's heir:
Though Antony treats him with condescension. [IV, i]
Brutus joins Cassius at Sardis, where
They both exhibit signs of pre-match tension . . . [IV, iii]

Soldiers need pay, and Cassius raised the lot
By taking bribes. Brutus is disgusted.
But Cassius knows what his great friend does not:
The world's corrupt, and no man can be trusted.

---

† 75 drachmas (then in circulation) —
I haven't made allowance for inflation.

The two are reunited; but the fight
Goes to Octavius and Mark Antony.
(Dead Caesar's ghost gave Brutus quite a fright
The night before — a sign of augury!) [IV, iii]

'This was the noblest Roman of them all.' [V, v, 68]
Mark Antony's much-quoted disquisition
Seems to regret his great opponent's fall —
But then, he was a clever politician!

King Henry IV
Part 1

'Give me a cup of sack, boy.' There's no prize [II, iv, 112]
For guessing who says this! Before our eyes
Stands Falstaff, loved by every generation
That's warmed to this spontaneous creation
Since he first creaked the boards beside the Thames
And made them merry with his stratagems.
His girth and mass impossible to guess;
Little in nothing; in everything excess;
His gravity (in the Newtonian sense)
Drawing the world to his circumference!
Asleep, insensible; awake, a child
Of needs immediate and urges wild;
The advocate and judge of his own cause;
Indifferent to censure or applause;
Perennially out of pocket . . . yet
His Richness leaves us ever in his Debt.

*

Henry IV, enthroned to wide acclaim,
Is still concerned that God has marked his name —

Richard II's downfall and demise
May well have damned him in celestial eyes.†
If serious debts of guilt have to be paid,
One cost-effective way is a Crusade; [I, i]
And he's been waiting for a year at least
To purge and stabilise the Middle East!
But news arrives that's positively
    alarming . . .
March and Northumberland have both
    been arming
Against the Welsh and Scots; and since they backed
King Richard, Henry fears *he'll* be attacked.
So obviously he's got to deal with them
Before his blood sports in Jerusalem!

*

That's Policy: now let us bare his Heart.
A private grief is tearing him apart . . .
Northumberland's renowned and
    urgent son,
Dubbed 'Hotspur', is admired by
    everyone,
Whereas Prince Hal, King Henry's
    flesh and blood,
Has dragged the royal image
    through the mud.

---

† You'll learn what happened in King Richard's play —
If you're in doubt, then read it right away.

We therefore move from the affairs of State [I, ii]
To where the Lower Orders congregate
In lodging-houses, inns and smoke-filled rooms,
Domain of landlords, tapsters, whores and grooms.
Meet Bardolph, Poins and Peto — three of those
Who, with Sir John, follow where Prince Hal goes
(Plus others who will later join the lists
Of those the Folio calls *Humourists*).
An escapade's in train, but we soon see
That this is part of Prince Hal's policy,
For as he tell us, when he's left alone, [I, ii, 190]
It's really preparation for the throne . . .
The wilder his youthful reputation
The more impressive his repudiation
When he is crowned! Falstaff & Co.
Arrange a theft, and Hal and Poins both go [II, iv]
To Gadshill, where it's planned — and, in disguise,
Scatter their friends, and make off with the prize . . .

Back to the plot. Hotspur is told to meet
The angry King about the non-receipt [I, iii]
Of prisoners he had been told to bring
For use in profitable ransoming —
The Treasury keeps its trading in the black
By selling all unwanted captives back.
Hotspur has kept them, and, on being rebuffed,
Tells Henry, in so many words, 'Get stuffed!'
The King decides to fix these Earls, and sends
For Hal, who is carousing with his friends.

This is the famous Boar's Head Tavern scene, [II, iv]
When Falstaff acts the King, asks where Hal's been,
And why he wastes his time with idle folk.
The topers are convulsed: but it's no joke
When Prince Hal plays the King. 'I banish you!'
He tells Sir John; and when we reach Part 2
And Hal is crowned, Falstaff *is* duly banned —
The change of heart the Prince had always planned.

*

The northern rebels meet. Owen Glendower,
The mighty Welshman, has attached his power
To that of March and Hotspur; they've begun [III, i]
To parcel England out before they've won!

Meanwhile King Henry leaves Hal in no doubt [III, ii]
It's time he got his image sorted out.
This is the Boar's Head jest, now played for real.
Hal's touched by Father's agonised appeal,
Says he'll reduce the clubbing and the booze,
And sort out Hotspur — which is welcome news.
Sir John has also, at the King's request,
A regiment of living scarecrows pressed . . .
The starved and derelict best suit his need —
There's less to hit, and also less to feed.

*

The rebel camp near Shrewsbury (Act Four): [IV, i]
They find they're minus half their troops or more . . .

Glendower's taking longer than he said;
Northumberland is tucked up in his bed;
But Hotspur's now on fire to get going,
Regardless of the troops the rest are owing —
The worse the odds, the greater the reward!
And anyway, he has to match his sword
With Hal, his deadly opposite and twin. [V, ii]
The embassies retire, and they begin . . . [V, iii]
No contest, really; nor is Henry's image
Improved by his performance in the scrimmage —
Knights in his habit serve as a distraction
To stop him being involved in too much action;
And when he *is*, Hal has to help him out.
The climax is our hero's mighty bout
With Hotspur, who declares from where he's lying
That loss of honour hurts him more than dying. [V, iv]
When Falstaff claims the kill, Hal doesn't mind . . .
In Part Two, though, he won't be quite so kind!

King Henry IV
Part 2

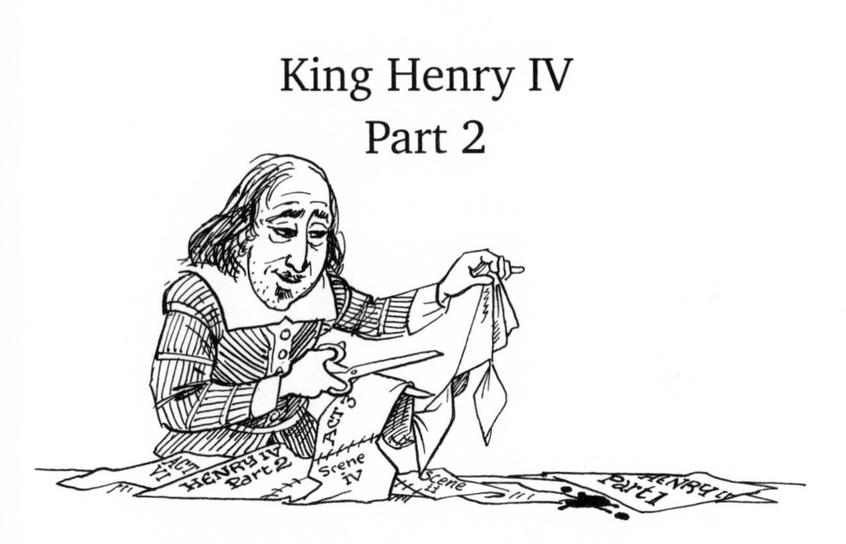

The second *Henry* comes off much the worst
When set beside the brilliance of the first
(The two plays have at times been shown as one,
Although a lot of cutting must be done,
With most of the excisions in this part!).
Assuming you have read Part 1, let's start
With the 'Induction' that begins the play,
When Rumour says that Hotspur won the day
At Shrewsbury, King Henry has been taken,
And Hal is dead! But Rumour is mistaken —
As we already know, Hotspur's been slain . . .
Can any of the rebels rise again?

*

A tiny scene (two minutes at the most) [Part I, IV, iv]
In Part 1, showed a rush to catch the post†
By York's Archbishop Scroop, with letters saying
He'll back the rebels, and do some extra praying.
Since then, we learn, he's thrown away his mitre,
Strapped on a sword, and turned into a fighter
For martyred Richard, thus bestowing grace
On Insurrection's unattractive face. 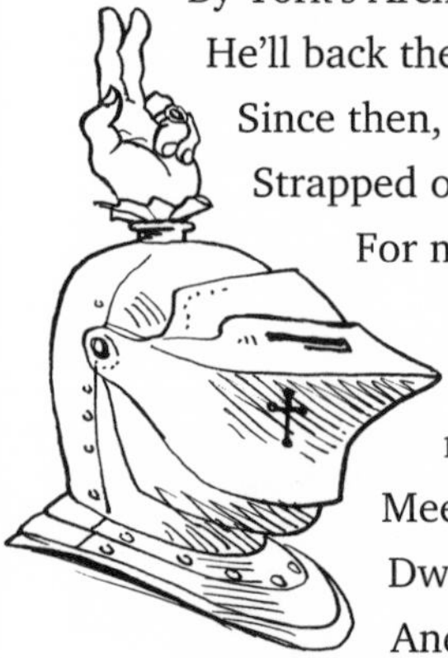
Bardolph, Mowbray and Hastings,
now in York, [I, iii]
Meet him and have an optimistic talk,
Dwelling on Henry's weakness at some length
And hoping it proves greater than their strength
(They skate over small problems of their own,
As one does when applying for a loan).

*

Meanwhile, Falstaff's come back from the war
As short of money as he was before, I, ii]
And now the Law is after him: we see
The Lord Chief Justice in his finery
Employed by Mistress Quickly, famed
hostess,
To make him pay her bill (the
tabloid press

---

† 'Sir Michael' took the sacred post away,
But isn't seen again in either play.

Is also trumpeting the latest scandal
In royal circles: Hal flew off the handle
And struck the Lord Chief Justice in a rage —
Though fortunately this occurred off-stage).
Falstaff and Quickly quickly put things right:
His whore Doll Tearsheet hopes he'll stay
the night,
But then he's ordered to proceed, post-haste,
To Yorkshire, where the new rebellion's based. [II, iv]
At Justice Shallow's Gloucestershire retreat
He stays for gossip and a bite to eat, [III, ii]
As well as to collect more ragged men
To march with him (it's like Part I again!).

*

King Henry's falling terminally ill.
He hopes that his Crusade may happen still,
But weighs the distance to the Holy Land
Against the level of his falling sand
(*Enter in nightgown* is the stage
direction). [III, i]
Hal's brother John defeats the
insurrection
At Gaultree Forest, by a
sleight-of-hand:
Archbishop Scroop and
his rebellious band

Are told the King will listen to their case
With sympathy: they drink a toast, embrace,
Dismiss their armies — and are led away
To pay the debt all traitors have to pay . . . [IV, ii]

*

Prince Hal, no party to this double-dealing,
Calls in to find out how his father's feeling.
The crown is placed beside the royal bed:
The King shows every sign of being dead [IV, v]
(Though really he's just taking forty winks);
And having now succeeded, as he thinks,
Hal takes the crown and goes off wearing it.
When Father finds it's gone, he has a fit.
Re-enter Hal: 'Dad, don't get in a state!
I wasn't — what's that word?
— *precipitate*.
Considering what the crown has
done for you,
I'm not sure that I want it!' (Is this true?)

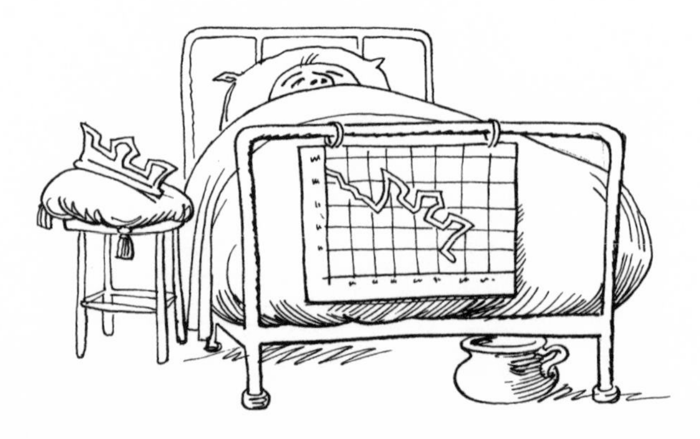

Well, anyway, since Henry's sinking quickly,
He murmurs some advice: 'The realm is sickly,
And you, my son, will naturally inherit
Much of my fault, and little of my merit.
There's still profound division in the State,
So what you need to do is to create
Some foreign quarrel, which will then unite
Our warring factions in the common fight.'
(A strategy of current usefulness
When the Economy is in a mess!)

*

So hapless Henry dies — and with him dies
The reckless Hal, who now transmogrifies
Into Henry V, the new-born Son, [V, ii]
Whose sudden majesty stuns everyone.
Falstaff is banned, although his ghost survives [V, iv]
In Shakespeare's pot-boiler, *The Merry Wives*;
But he has disappeared from Hal's domain . . .
The Superstar now starts his famous reign!

King Henry V

Henry the Fifth is too good to be true:
There's absolutely nothing he can't do
(Except speak French, when he sets out to win
The dowry of Princess Katharine).
The Prologue thunders: 'O for a Muse of fire!'
What note could raise our expectation higher?
Heroic treatment of its martial theme;
A warrior king and his Imperial dream;
The proud resurgence of a mighty nation
Seared by the flame of civil conflagration,
United by a piece of Gallic cheek —
The details of which I'll later speak.

*

As you'd expect, it's fairly black-and-white —
The French are always wrong, the English right!
Henry decides to challenge France's throne,
Believing it is his and his alone;
The Archbishop of Canterbury proves [I, ii]
His ownership (at several removes),
Although the French insist that Salic Law
Debars him — hence the reason for the war.†

---

† 'The Law says only males may pass on a royal name,
But Henry's *female* line is used to justify his claim.

At this point, French ambassadors appear,
To tell them, with a diplomatic sneer,
That Hal had better stay at home and play —
Here are some balls to pass the time
away!
This insult heats the blood and
heightens ardour:
Ships strain their ropes, and
blacksmiths hammer harder, 
Beating and tempering each glowing blade
And nailing horses to the shoes they've made.
As through a microscope, we also see
One drop enlarged, of this confederacy: [II, i]
The Boar's Head Tavern humourists we knew
From Henry's father's tale (Parts 1 and 2) —
Bardolph and Pistol, joined by Corporal Nym;
But as for Falstaff, all we hear of him
Is told by Mistress Quickly . . . that he died [II, iii]
In her house, at the turning of the tide,
His heart congealed by the King's
unkindness.

Over the Channel, we hear His Royal Highness [II, iv]
The Dauphin (heir of France) assure the lords
They'll make the English dance upon their swords!

*

The next part of the play, Acts 3 and 4,
Describe the major battles of the war —
Harfleur and Agincourt. Henry's great speech
Which opens thus: 'Once more unto the breach!' [III, i, 1]
(Widely anthologized) is stirring
stuff,
But Bardolph and his kin have
had enough . . . [III, ii]
Enter four comic Captains, a
selection
From Henry's multi-national
collection,
Who show how much his
charisma has done
To turn the island races
into one.

With Harfleur fallen, Katharine tries (and fails)
To learn the English word for 'fingernails' — [III, iv, 45]
If things go on like this, she has a hunch
That Henry will be turning up for lunch.
But now the army plans to stop him short
By full-frontal assault at Agincourt.

*

The greatest set-piece Shakespeare ever wrote?
The Battle of Agincourt's famous for its quote
'We few, we happy few, we band of brothers'; [IV, iii, 60]
But this is one line among many others
That make Act 4 such a delight to read
(So much slides past, delivered at the speed
Of dialogue, that there's no other way
Of grasping everything he has to say).
In Scene 1, for the only time, we hear
King Henry musing with nobody near
About his guilt for Richard, and the weight

Of cares that toss and turn the Bed of State . . .
But, come great morning, he's himself again.
His Crispin's Day address inspires his men,
Who massacre ten thousand, which seems plenty:
The fallen English come to nine and twenty. [IV, viii]
So back to England . . . God's will was surely done —
Through him and him alone the fight was won!

*

Henry returns to France: the treaty's signed,
And Katharine is finally resigned [V, ii]
To learning English.† The Chorus then explains
How things go downhill when their offspring reigns . . .
So, very soon, this Superstar will be
A bright and never-fading memory!

---

† *Henry*. O fair Katharine, if you will love me soundly with your French heart, I will be glad to hear you confess it brokenly with your English tongue. [V, ii, 104]

King Henry VI Part 1

Including the Meteoric Career of
Joan of Arc (*La Pucelle*)
and the Origin of the Wars of the Roses

This trilogy contains some early plays.
The Superstar, Henry the Fifth, is dead;
Old wounds re-open, and the turbulent days
Of his son's feeble tenure lie ahead.
Do not expect the text to match the stuff
That Shakespeare would eventually write —
Though most of it is competent enough,
He didn't achieve greatness overnight!

One reason why these plays have not done better
(They're very rarely seen
upon the stage)
Is learning who is who,
in the theatre —
It's less confusing on
the printed page!
The Tudors, being closer to
those times,
Knew these events and
people inside-out;

But if you study the ensuing rhymes,
You'll get a taste of what they're all about!

The King was one when his doomed reign began,
So Lord Protector Gloucester kept things running;
But Richard of York has now begun to plan
How he could win the crown by being cunning.
This is the background to the Roses Wars,
Which all the land will soon be passing through:
But foreign troubles will delay the cause
Of kingmaking until we reach Part 2 . . .

The conquered French have started to regain
Their hijacked lands. The mighty Talbot tries
To win usurped Orleans back again,
And almost does: which predicates the rise
Of Joan of Arc ('*Pucelle*' is rather rude)† —
A shepherd's daughter, hence of humble stock,
Who claims with Mary's grace to be imbued,
And gives the English army quite a shock. [I, ii & iv-vi]

Orleans is won back in the second Act
By Talbot; but there's fighting
all the time

† It can refer to virtue or to vice:
Applied to Joan it isn't very nice.

Until, at last, Angiers is attacked,
And Joan, tied to the stake, is made sublime. [V, iii & iv]
This lady is extremely energetic,
In various beds as well as in the field;
Her image, therefore, is
unsympathetic —
One reason why this piece has not
appealed.

Now, having let too many years
go by,
We must retrace our temporal strides, and see
The Temple Gardens scene, where voices high
Dispute some points of Genealogy. [II, iv]
King Henry's line from Lancaster comes down,
While Richard hails from the House of York . . .
Which one has greater right to England's crown?
This is what prompts such animated talk.

Richard, insisting that York's claim is higher,
Sneers at Lancastrians like Somerset,
Whips out his secateurs, and from a briar
Cuts for his buttonhole a White rosette.
The others follow suit (they're well equipped):
Richard's fans choosing White, the others Red,
Thus showing their favour by the blooms they've snipped
(Make sure this colour-coding's in your head!).

The Lord Protector's basically nice,
And thinks that kindly favours are returned:
But now he gives the King unwise advice. [III, i]
'Your cousin Richard, in my view, has earned
Some recognition. Why not take your sword
And make him Duke of York?' 'A good idea!
It's time he had his ducal seat restored!'
The White Rose blossoms . . . war is coming near . . . †

*

Now back to France, where Margaret (the
daughter
Of Anjou's Duke) is forcibly induced [V, iii]
To marry Henry. Ordered to escort her,
The Duke of Suffolk is at once seduced
Both by her beauty and the chance
she'll bring
To get the country's business in his grip
By being master both of her and King. [V, iv]
But, as he ought to know, there's many a slip . . .

---

† Henry V declared the title dead —
Yorkists were planning to remove his head!
A hint, at least, that his son might be wise
To let it lie, rather than help it rise.

King Henry VI
Part 2

The Rise and Fall of the Duke of Suffolk,
Queen Margaret's Lover;
The Bloody Rebellion of Jack Cade;
and the Duke of York's Victory at St Albans

	ROSA GALLICA (*The Reds*)	*ROSA ALBA* (*The Whites*)
MANAGER	King Henry VI	Richard, Duke of York
STAR PLAYERS	Duke of Suffolk	Earl of Salisbury
	Duke of Somerset	Earl of Warwick
	Duke of Buckingham	

Referee: Duke of Gloucester

Meet Margaret of Anjou, King Henry's Queen —
The biggest female role the Bard would write.
A pity that she's hardly ever seen . . .
Within this trilogy, she's out of sight!

No other part in Shakespeare would extend
Across four plays in all . . . from bartered bride
Till shrivelled, grey, and halfway round the bend,
She curses Richard Crookback, regicide.†

The handsome Duke of Suffolk's great ambition
(To rule the King, as he rules Margaret)
Is barred by Gloucester's dominant position
As Lord Protector. Hopeful Somerset
And Buckingham also wish Gloucester dead
To clear *their* royal path; and though these three
Are all Lancastrians, and all wear Red,
There's not much evidence of harmony!

*

So jealousy begins to blight the Rose
Of Lancaster, King Henry's troubled seat;
And, seeing this, the Opposition knows
It's time to move. Salisbury and Warwick meet
With Richard, Duke of York: they feel their hour

---

† In *Richard III*, IV, iv

Has almost come: they'll crush this squabbling lot,
And, having won the fight for Flower Power,
Plant *Rosa alba* † firmly in the pot!

The wife of Gloucester does her level best [I, ii]
(A foretaste of Macbeth, you must agree!)
To plant Ambition in his noble breast.
With spirits she consorts, whose prophecy [I, iv]
Of others' doom, unwisely written down,

Leads to her trial, judgement, and proscription [II, iii]
(Trudging in sackcloth barefoot through the town), [II, iv]
And means the end of Gloucester's job description!

*

† Latin for *White Rose* (known as Yorkshire's Rose even today);
While *Rosa gallica*, the red the opposition chose,
Means Rose of France. This was employed in medicine, by the way —
And therefore bears the charming name 'Apothecary's Rose'.

The King decides that Suffolk has to go.
He's dangerous, and needs to be transported —
But Margaret's tearful
    protestations show
That she and he have secretly
    cavorted!
The sundered lovers share a
    last embrace
Before he has to hurry off and pack;
It is their last encounter face to face,
Although she does get one bit of him back . . . [IV, iv]

The Mob! To Shakespeare, they're an untuned string,
Which skilful words can wind to such a tension
That they're amenable to anything.
Richard of York's unsociable intention
To make all London's working classes rise [III, i]
And topple helpless Henry, needs the aid
Of someone skilled in such an enterprise —
A clothier, in fact! His name's Jack Cade.

To start with, everything is going right,
And Richard, with his cavalry, prepares
To march in when disorder's at its height
And grasp the baffled crown . . . Jack Cade declares
That privilege and wealth must be uprooted; [IV, ii-viii]
All courts of law, all seats of learning sacked;
All speakers of the French tongue executed;
Free ale, free food, free everything in fact . . .

. . . but like all parties, they run out of booze!
King Henry softens them with guarantees;
Cade wins them back; they hesitate, then choose
The King. 'Feathers swirl straighter than the likes of these!'
Cade grumbles: 'What a vacillating bunch!' [IV, viii, 55]
He picks some lettuce from a garden bed [IV, x]
To make a summer salad for his lunch.
The owner spots him, and cuts
off his head.

While on the subject of Decapitation,
The Duke of Suffolk's own head was removed
En route for France, just after embarkation. [IV, i]

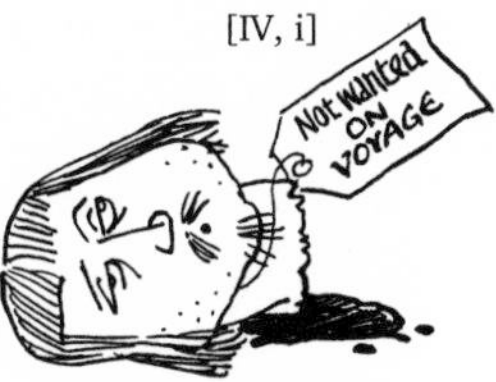

Posted to Margaret, it has not improved
Her marital relationship one bit;
For it will go off if it's not kept cool,
But she keeps wandering around with it,
And calls her royal spouse a gutless fool . . . [IV, iv]

The Duke of Somerset now wields the power
That keeps the Yorkists from King Henry's crown.
The Reds pretend the Duke is in the Tower, [V, i]
So Richard tells his army to stand down,
Imagining that Henry will concede;
But realises that he has been outwitted
When Somerset's dramatically freed!
And so to battle both sides are committed . . .

The Battle of St Albans ends this play. [V, ii]
We get the feeling that the Whites have won;
But, as Part 3 will make clear right away,
The Roses Wars have only just begun.
Early retirement would suit the King —
He'd love a life of gentle contemplation;
But *that's* not likely to be happening
With Margaret out for total domination!

King Henry VI
Part 3

The Abject Resignation of King Henry;
Queen Margaret's Campaign on behalf of her Son, Prince Edward;
and the crowning of Edward Duke of York
as Edward IV

	ROSA GALLICA *(The Reds)*	*ROSA ALBA* *(The Whites)*
MANAGERS	Queen Margaret	Richard, Duke of York
		Edward (Edward IV)
STAR PLAYERS	Lord Clifford	Richard (Richard III)
	Duke of Somerset	

Promoter: Earl of Warwick

The Battle of St Albans runs its course.
Enter the Whites, boasting of whom they slew [I, i]
In overcoming Henry's desperate force
(Though he's still technically King, it's true).

The throne is empty. Richard of York sits down;
The King comes in and does a double-take.
'*That's my place*!' 'No it's not. Give up your crown.
Swear fealty for dead King Richard's sake.'

My claim *is* weak, thinks Henry. What to do?
He says: 'Look here, would you mind hanging on
Until I'm dead? I'll pass it on to you
And all your heirs, I promise!' Whereupon
Queen Margaret marches in, her bosom heaving,
Prince Edward with her, clinging to her skirt.
'If you don't take that back again, I'm leaving!
Our son is going to reign, you little squirt!'

Phew! Now we know who's in the driving seat!
She, Clifford and Northumberland
won't rest
Until the House of York is at
their feet.
(A word about Lord Clifford,
who's obsessed
With Retribution — in the
previous play [Part 2, V, ii]
York killed his father,
and the son admits

His one aim is to put the Duke away
And chop his children into little bits.)

The Duke is captured: in a famous scene [I, iv]
He's crowned with paper, mocked and vilified
By the relentless and vindictive Queen . . .
'O tiger's heart wrapp'd in a woman's hide!' [I, iv, 137]
He cries as he is stabbed and left to bleed,
His youngest child's blood smeared on his face
(Lord Clifford carried out this vengeful deed —
The whole thing is an absolute disgrace).

Margaret & Co. are hoping to be thanked
When Henry's shown York's amputated head; [II, ii]
But since he thought their charter sacrosanct
He's most upset, and starts to cry instead.
They order him to keep out of the way,
And so he famously soliloquises
On how he'd much prefer to spend
each day
In simple nine-to-five, with no surprises!

The Duke of York's heir, Edward,
seizes power [II, vi]
At Towton. Margaret flees
without her crown,

The prayerful Henry's musing in
the Tower,
And you might think that things will
settle down.
But no! King Edward's in a silly mess
Of his own making. He meets
Lady Grey, [III, ii]
A widow, whom he's anxious to possess.
She says: 'Unless you marry me — no way!'

Warwick is working for this Casanova [III, iii]
To fix a marriage with the French king's sister:
This merry widow business bowls him over —
He tells exiled Queen Margaret he'll assist her

In sending the inconstant fellow packing!
Edward is kidnapped, camping out one night, [IV, iii]
And Henry once more crowned, with Warwick's
backing . . . [IV, vi]
Two kings he's raised — one Red, the other White!†

EPILOGUE

The End? Not quite, for if you know your Past,
You'll be aware that Henry doesn't last.
Edward, with massive forces, takes control:
At Tewksbury important heads will roll,
Including that of Henry's only son. [V, v]
King Henry's faltering race is also run,
Stabbed in the Tower (although this crowning act
Does not accord with documented fact)
By Crookback Richard, who has
made it plain [III, ii]
That brother Edward's heirs aren't
going to reign . . .
He wants the throne himself, as
we shall see
When he is crowned as
Richard No. 3!

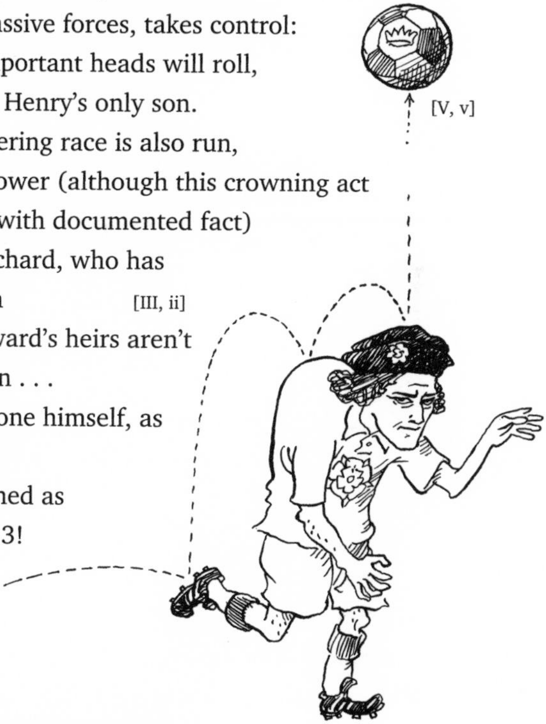

† The Kingmaker is how he's known today;
But king-making's a dangerous game to play.

King John

King John has a troublesome reign.
His lands stretch from Ireland to Spain —
But during this play
Half are given away,
And England's invaded again!

It begins with a high-level meeting . . . [I, i]
An envoy from France brings a greeting,
And then says that the crown
Should have been handed down
To John's nephew — so John has been cheating.

Young Arthur, this claimant by law,†
Has a mother who's now urging war
To give him the lands
That should be in his hands
(He's so sweet, that he's frankly a bore).

---

† His father was John's elder brother,
Who is, sadly, no longer around. . .
So there's no doubt that he, and no other,
Is the true heir, and should have been crowned.

John's own mother's a force
  to be reckoned —
The widow of Henry the Second,
Named Eleanor, who
A dispassionate view
Must dismiss as disastrously
  fecund . . .

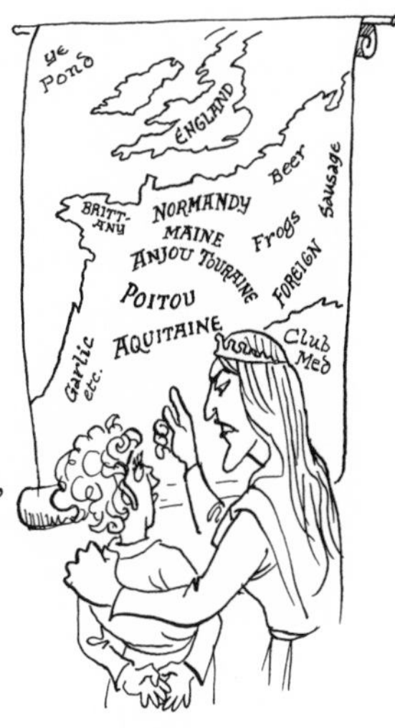

Four sons (to their parents' dismay!),
All seeking the crown, come
  what may —
King John, last and least,
Is a positive beast,
And doesn't *deserve* his own play.

Though Eleanor knows that his claim
Is much weaker than Arthur's in name,
She tells him to fight,
Since Possession gives Right —
And King John thinks exactly the same!

John's brother, King Richard (well-known
For an excess of Testosterone),
Had fathered a son
Who by now has begun
To dispute how much land he
  should own.

King John takes the Bastard to heart
(That's the name he has, right from the start).
His mordant perspective
Is highly effective —
It is, without doubt, the star part!

The folk of the town of Angiers [II, i]
Are almost prostrated with fear
When the French come in sight;
Then (a still bigger fright)
King John and his Mother appear . . .

The armies dispute, but in vain,
So with no territorial gain
(Although both sides score,
The result is a draw),
They decide to divide the domain . . .

To ensure a perpetual peace,
John will hand a convenient niece
To the Dauphin, plus gold,
Plus five duchies all told,
So that Arthur's contention will cease!

The boy's mother reviews the position.
It seems like the end of her mission; [III, i]
But a chap from the Pope
Rekindles her hope
By sending John's soul to Perdition . . .

The reason Rome gives
him the sack
Is his utter refusal to back
The churchman they pick
For the Archbishopric . . .
So the French turn around, and attack!

John's men do remarkably well
Considering he's destined for Hell . . . [III, iv]
Young Arthur is seized
(So his mother's displeased),
And we find him confined in a cell. [IV, i]

Arthur sweet-talks the warder, and since
He's a kind man, he unbars the prince,
Who's then killed in a fall
From the top of a wall — [IV, iii]
The scene does not always
convince.

So it's really just Gravity's force
That leads to this rapid divorce
Between Country and King —
For they're all reckoning
That John must have pushed him, of course!

No one is prepared to prevent
The Dauphin's troops landing in Kent;
And though it's a wrench,
Some lords join with the French
To show John that it's high time he went! [V, ii]

A bug leaves the King feeling low,
So the Bastard takes charge
of the show;
And the nobles who tried
To unseat John, decide
They'll return to the devil
they know . . . [V, iv]

King John dies, leaving Henry, his son —
So with luck they are back to Square One. [V, vii]
The country's about
To throw the French out . . .
And with this happy prospect, we're done!

King Lear

The burden of admin makes King Lear declare [I, i]
That he'll give his domain to his daughters
(Each ruling one part), and then, free of all care,
He'll carouse with his knights and supporters.

The apportionment's done by a novel device:
His three daughters are given a test
That matches the richness and size of their slice
To the filial love each professed.

That's the theory, at least: but in
fact we soon see
That Cordelia's slated to win;
So that Regan and Goneril, older
than she,
Are the losers before they begin!

But he's shocked when Cordelia doesn't exceed
Her sisters' excesses. She states:
'I love you, of course; but no more, I concede,
Than our mutual bonding dictates.

'Both my sisters have husbands. It's bare-faced deceit
To pretend so much passion for you . . .
When I marry, my husband will be in receipt
Of all the affection he's due!'

Is she right in incurring her father's displeasure,
Instead of just doing her stuff?
Like cool Isabella in *Measure for Measure*,
Is she simply not human enough?

King Lear goes ballistic, but Kent intervenes:†
'She's just being honest,
you know —
Unlike her two sisters,
she's said what she
means.'
'Clear off!' roars the king.
'You're *de trop*!'

† The level-headed Duke of Kent
Endures much disparagement.

Undowered, she might have been left on the shelf:
But the King of France takes her as Queen,
Seeing riches unmined in the lady herself —
Though he vanishes after this scene.

So now let us turn to the parallel plot, [I, ii]
Which concerns the unequal position
Of Gloucester's son Edgar, who's rightly begot,
And his bastard son Edmund's ambition . . .

Edgar cooks Edmund's goose with the ludicrous claim
That he wants Father's title and lands;
So the true son's deprived of his
fortune and name,
Which are now in his
half-brother's hands!

Both Edgar and Kent have
been outlawed, and play
Indispensable parts, as you'll see:
While King Lear, with his Fool and
his knights, goes to stay
With Goneril (Act 1 Scene 3).

These undisciplined guests make a terrible mess, [I, iv]
And I don't think his daughter's to blame

For ordering Father to curb their excess . . .
If they stayed with me, I'd do the same!

(The fact that he suffers, goes mad, is redeemed,
And dies of a mortified heart,
Shouldn't make us forget how unpleasant he seemed
When he misbehaved right at the start.)

With terrible curses, he goes off to stay
With Regan and Cornwall (her lord);
But they're warned by her sister, and hurry away
To where Gloucester does bed and full board. [II, i]

Kent has gone there disguised (he is serving
King Lear,
As he will till the end of the plot); [II, ii]
Then the monarch and Goneril also appear . . .
So poor Gloucester's now feeding the lot. [II, iv]

Both sisters, united, face Father's request
To allow him more knights in his train.
The one who permits him the most, loves him best —
It's Act 1 Scene 1 over again!

Fifty knights? Twenty? Ten? Five? The numbers decline
As this grotesque Dutch auction proceeds . . .
Regan snaps: 'What needs *one*?' which prompts Lear's
famous line:
'A beggar has more than he needs!' [II, iv, 266]

At this critical juncture, the storm will begin.
Disillusioned, he's starting to wonder
What is left of a man when he's stripped to the skin,
When we hear the first peals of thunder . . .

Kent, helped by the Fool (who is mordantly wise),
Keeps the mad king as dry as he can. [III, ii]
And Edgar appears in the naked disguise
Of Poor Tom — Lear's exemplary man. [III, iv]

Regan's husband puts out Gloucester's eyes
(quite a sight!). [III, vii]
He tells Poor Tom, who offers a hand:
'Find a cliff-top near Dover, of towering height.
Then I'll jump — I've had all I can stand!' [IV, i, 73]

His unrecognised son engineers the illusion
When Gloucester believes he descends
To his death, but is saved by the
helpful collusion
Of Providence, making amends . . . [IV, vi]

Now to the Reunion (Act 4 Scene 7).
Lear awakes, his convulsions abated,
And Cordelia seems like an angel from heaven
Instead of the daughter he hated!

The other two sisters fall out with each other.
They've gone down with Edmund to Dover,
Both greatly enamoured of Edgar's half-brother . . .
Which one will he choose when it's over? [V, i]

The French troops don't put up a very good show, [V, iii]
So Lear and his daughter are caught.
But Edgar calls Edmund a traitor, and so
A duel will have to be fought!

Edmund falls, and the sisters who
    fancied his charms
Reach their own self-determined demise.
Enter Lear, with Cordelia dead in his arms —
Does he think she still lives, when he dies?†

† *Lear*. Thou'lt come no more,
Never, never, never, never, never.
Pray you undo this button. Thank you, sir.
Do you see this? Look on her. Look, her lips.
Look there, look there! *He dies.* [V, iii, 307]

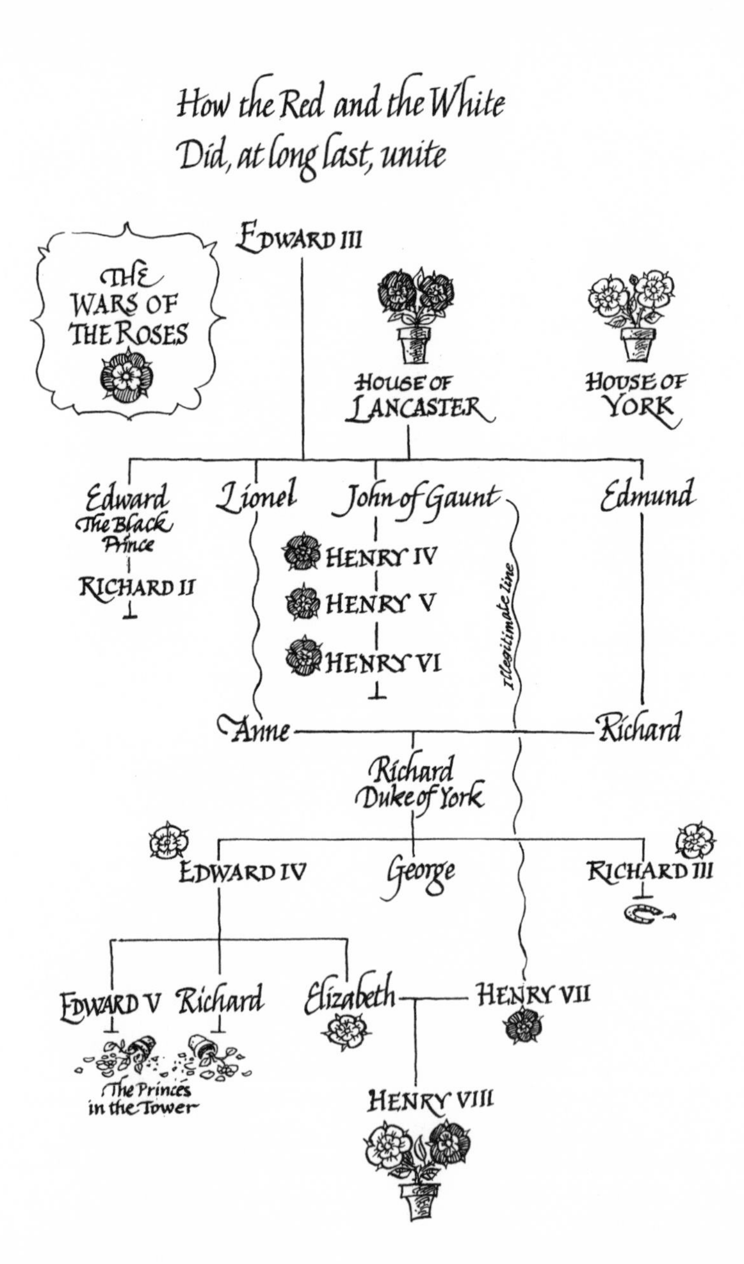
How the Red and the White
Did, at long last, unite
THE WARS OF THE ROSES
EDWARD III
HOUSE OF LANCASTER
HOUSE OF YORK
Edward The Black Prince
RICHARD II
Lionel
John of Gaunt
Edmund
HENRY IV
HENRY V
HENRY VI
Illegitimate line
Anne
Richard
Richard Duke of York
EDWARD IV
George
RICHARD III
EDWARD V
Richard
Elizabeth
HENRY VII
The Princes in the Tower
HENRY VIII

King Richard II

King Richard's story is the key
To most of Shakespeare's history:
What happened in these turbulent days
Prefigures all the 'Henry' plays —
The kings that John of Gaunt would start.
His son (the second biggest part)
Is Henry Bolingbroke, who'll be
Henry IV, as we shall see,
When Richard's forced to abdicate.
But this is to anticipate . . .
To start with, he is Richard's friend:
We see him fearlessly contend
That Thomas Mowbray is a traitor . . . [I, i]
They meet to fight a few weeks later, [I, iii]

But after all the heralding
King Richard steps into the ring
And banishes them, there and then!
Henry gets six years (down from ten
Since John of Gaunt kicks up a fuss
And says that ten's ridiculous);
While Mowbray gets a one-way ticket,
Complaining that it isn't cricket —
And who knows what those people thought
Who trudged for miles to watch the sport!

*

Gaunt now propounds his jaundiced view
Of what the place is coming to
With Richard in the driving seat
(Self-loving, whimsical, effete,
Lacking in majesty and grace) . . .
England has forfeited her place
As leader of the meekly led,

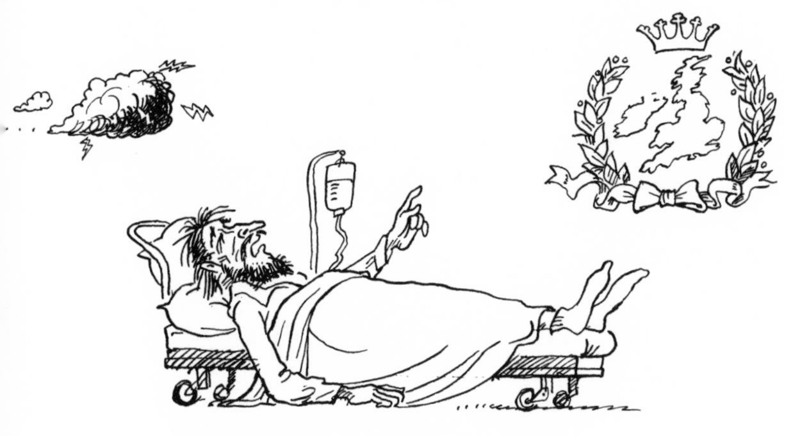

And has to bow to them instead![†]
'To run your Court from day to day
You've mortgaged everything away.
Murder, corruption, overspending —
I'm glad my lease of life is ending!' [II, i]

*

I think old Gaunt is meant to be
The mouthpiece of Posterity,
Since minutes later he is dead —
Which gives some force to what he's said.
Now Richard makes his biggest blunder.
The Irish still won't knuckle under,
And so he needs to raise a force.
But how to pay for it? *Of course*!
Careless of what this may provoke,
The lands of Henry Bolingbroke

† *Gaunt*. This royal throne of kings, this sceptered isle. . .
Is now leased out — I die pronouncing it —
Like to a tenement, or pelting farm. [II, i, 40-60]

(Who's now inherited the title)
Are sold. Henry demands requital,
Sails his forces up the Humber, [II, iii]
And troops too numerous to number
Join in the lengthening procession
To challenge Richard's repossession
Of what by right is Henry's own.
It seems a challenge to the throne:
The Duke of York, trying to be
An unofficial referee
(Since he's the uncle of them both)
Asks Henry to respect the oath
That on his banishment he took.
But Henry has an answer. 'Look.
I've gained my father's seat — the vow
I took as heir can't bind me now.
I simply want to get my hands
On my appropriated lands!'

*

Richard has gone to fight the wars
In Ireland, which were the cause
Of all this fuss. When he gets back
He finds things looking pretty black — [III, ii]
Henry is in the driving seat!
Richard's acceptance of defeat
Is garnished with a certain measure
Of almost masochistic pleasure.

'What must the king do now? he sighs. [III, iii, 143]
'Must he submit?' In Henry's eyes
Richard is still anointed king —
But having mucked up everything,
Should he still be allowed to rule
When he is clearly such a fool?
This is the crisis of the play:
Can mortal judges really say
A king should be removed by force?
This will be Henry's cross, of course!

*

King Richard neither yields nor fights:
He simply loses all his rights! [IV, i]
The people show their discontent
By pelting him with excrement;† [V, ii]

† It's given as 'dust and rubbish' in the play
But this is my conclusion, anyway!

And in his cell, there's time at last
To ponder his unhappy past: [V, v]
How clearly he sees everything
Without the trappings of a king!

*

Though Henry has already said
He'd like this awkward fellow dead,
He gets the ultimate of shocks
To see him, murdered, in a box. [V. vi]
'For this deed, God will punish me —
How to amend such blasphemy?'
The 'Henry' plays show how this crime
Will haunt the crown for quite some time!

King Richard III

There's not much finesse
Behind Richard's success;
Nor is he reluctant to say
How his long-term ambition
Will achieve its fruition
(To be Richard the Third, come what may).

In the York legacy
He's the youngest of three.
The oldest one, Edward, is crowned;
So he needs a pretext
To kill George, who is next —
And make sure that no heirs are around!

Now I'm fully aware
Of the sense of despair
Felt by people who've taken the view
That Shakespeare's distortion
Is a monstrous abortion —
And a re-vamp is long overdue.

But he left us this play,
And it won't go away;
So I'll open my rhyming rendition
With Richard of Gloucester
Determined to foster
A measure of sibling suspicion! [I, i]

King Edward's upset.
Richard claims there's a threat
That endangers the future succession . . .
Brother George plans a coup
(Which of course isn't true)
So that *his* line will be in possession!

Edward puts George in clink,
Where he's challenged to drink
Rather more than the guidelines suggest. [I, iv]
So with George marinated,
And his heirs relocated,
The young Princes must now be suppressed . . .

Richard first plans to woo
The widowed Anne, who
Married Henry VI's son and heir.
Now she follows the coffin
Of King Henry (bumped off in
The Tower) in utter despair! [I, ii]

Knowing Richard killed both,
Anne's predictably loath
To say Yes: but his case is prepared.
'*You're* the one I desired!
All my crimes *you* inspired!
If we marry, our guilt will be shared!'†

King Edward is dead
(Over-sexed, over-fed). [II, ii]
His in-laws (the Queen's kith and kin)
Are determined to own
The heirs to the throne —
So Richard decides to move in . . .

His friend Buckingham, who
Has preferment in view,
Helps to get Edward's sons in his power. [II, iv]

---

† *Richard*. Was ever woman in this humour wooed?
Was ever woman in this humour won? [I,ii,228]

Richard takes the top ends
Off their uncles and friends, [III, iii]
And puts the two lads in the Tower.†

He now has it said
(And the word will soon spread)
That the Princes cannot be called Regal . . .
King Edward was not
By his father begot —
And his marriage was also illegal! [III, vii]

If this really is so,
Then the crown ought to go
To himself, who is next in the queue.
But the *hoi polloi* say:
'Ruled by Gloucester? No way!'
So Buckingham says what to do . . .

'You need to appear
Devout and sincere.
Hold this prayer-book, and
say that you'd be
Quite useless as king —
It's the very last thing
You would dream of . . .
then leave it to me!'

---

†Edward, 12 and Richard, 10.
Never seen alive again. . .

As you'll no doubt have guessed
They are greatly impressed —
His refusal is hard to resist.
So they start saying 'Please!'
Till they're down on their knees . . .
And he tells them: 'Oh — if you insist!'

But it's secretly said [IV, iii]
That the Princes are dead;
And it's clear that King Richard's to blame.
Henry Tudor's the one
In whose line they've begun
To believe, though he
hasn't much claim!

Henry starts his advance,
Coming over from France
To enjoy the last Act of the play. [V, ii]

The King's army is greater,
And Tudor's a traitor . . .
Of course he will win on The Day!

But a spectral tableau
By the ones he laid low
Gives King Richard a hell of a fright, [V, iii]
And tells Henry he's won
Long before they've begun
(So why on earth bother to fight?).

The day runs its course; [V, iv]
Richard's stuck for a horse,†
And everyone's really delighted
That Bosworth's decision
Heals England's division . . .
Foes no more, but Old
Friends Reunited! [V, v]

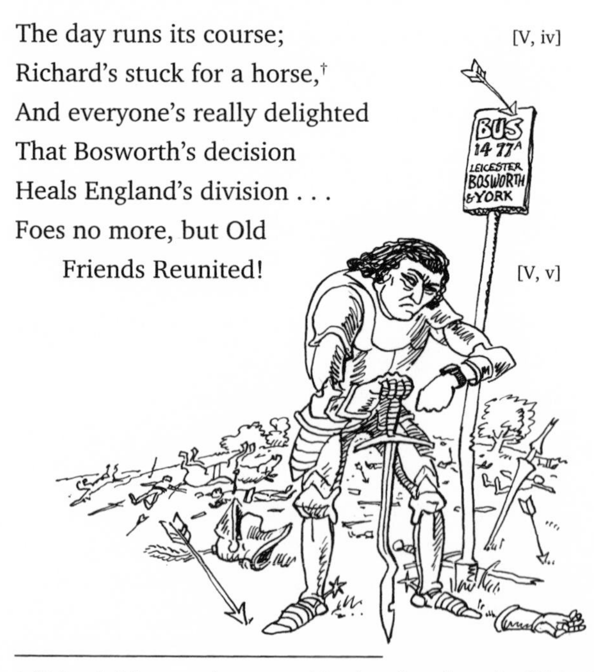

† *Richard.* A horse, a horse, my kingdom for a horse! [V, iv, 13]

Love's Labour's Lost

Love's Labour's Lost can mystify our modern generation —
There's even some debate about the title's punctuation!
Should 'Labours' just be plural, or apostrophized (possessive)?
I won't go further into this, in case I seem obsessive,
But if you start to read the text, you'll rapidly find out
That WORDS (punned, mangled, mispronounced) are what this
play's about.

*

I'll tell you what the story is, before we go too far.
King Ferdinand, the ruler of the French realm of Navarre
Involves three of his nobles in a most unlikely
scheme
To spend three years of study in the
Groves of Academe. [I, i]
A punishing routine of work and fast and
self-denial
And not a single female to come within
one mile!

A French Princess arrives with three Attendants
in her train, [II, i]
But they learn that their attempt to gain admission is in vain;
So these four undaunted ladies set up camp beyond the gate —
Their presence the Academy will discombobulate.
What's lacking, to a modern mind, is any sort of *plot*.
Nor does the action ever leave the same unlabelled spot
Where sometimes men, more often ladies, seem to be in charge
In games of verbal tennis or exchanging badinage.

That, in a nutshell, is this courtly frolic's *mise en scène*:
Four witty ladies making sport with four distracted men
Of whom the most articulate is someone called Berowne
(In addition there's a Constable, a Curate and a Clown,

A Schoolmaster a Spaniard — Don
Armado — and a Page,
Who all assassinate the English language
on the stage).
Berowne, at the beginning, says he's
doubtful of the plan —
To renounce both wine and women is too
much for any man —
But though he joins the others when they
swear the oath and sign,
He's the first to get embroiled, when he
falls for Rosaline,
And pays the Clown to carry her his
written declaration
(Which stimulates reflections on the word
Remuneration).

[III, i, 129-169]

*

Is Rosaline a sketch for the Dark Lady, who appears
In the Sonnets, also written in our poet's early years?
It's not unlikely, for he never wrote another play
That contains such clear allusions to the topics of the day,
Such as Walter Ralegh's coterie, here called the School
of Night; [IV, iii]
While for Ferdinand read Henri, then a Protestant,
whose fight

To clinch his claim to France's throne was backed by
Good Queen Bess
(Though once he changed his faith, the Virgin liked him
rather less).

*

Will's genius has kept him fresh — a Poet for All Time:
But in *Love's Labour's Lost*, for once, his densely written rhyme
Has seemed to many not far short of verbal diarrhoea,
So cuts are made and speeches slashed — whole scenes
may disappear!
Attempts to stage this comedy in a persuasive manner
Have damaged reputations; and even Kenneth Branagh
Got slated by the critics, although Trevor Nunn fared better
With his last Shakespeare production at the National Theatre.
To warn you, here's a Latin verb the Clown speaks,
rendered thus:
H O N O R I F I C A B I L I T U D I N I T A T I B U S ! †

† 'Ready to be honoured' [V, i, 42]

Macbeth

Equivocation is the key
To this most tragic history . . .
Perplexing ambiguity
Will undermine Macbeth.

Fire burn and cauldron bubble . . .
Visions causing endless trouble . . .
Everything appearing double —
Especially to Macbeth.

Three Weird Sisters in Scene 1 . . .
Witches known to everyone —
Even those who've never done
A project on *Macbeth*!

They drop a hint when they declare:
'Fair is foul, and foul is fair';
They're working out exactly where
They're going to meet Macbeth . . .

Our hero, meanwhile, has fought
Encounters of a bloody sort.
We hear an eye-witness report [I, ii]
Of how the 'brave Macbeth'

Rallied the Scotsmen to suppress
Norwegian avariciousness
With most conspicuous success.
He enters (out of breath) [I, iii]

With Banquo, who's as puffed as he,
For both fought energetically,
And are confronted by the Three,
Who all salute Macbeth

As Thane of Cawdor ('Which I'm not!');
Soon to be crowned ('What utter rot!');
But further kings will be begot
Of Banquo, not Macbeth!

Two fellow-noblemen appear,
With news that makes one forecast clear:
The Thane of Cawdor's end is near —
He'll meet a traitor's death . . .

And as a well-deserved reward,
King Duncan's going to award

The forfeit title of this lord
To trustworthy Macbeth!

This quite unnerving
precognition
Is what inspires his Ambition
To occupy the Top Position;
He sends Lady Macbeth

By first-class post
a resumé [I, v]
Of what the Witches had to say.
'You will rule Scotland, come what may!'
Avows Lady Macbeth.

King Duncan asks them if he might
Stay at their castle for a night.
'I'll drug his bodyguards — all right?'
His wife says to Macbeth. [I, vii]

He's basically horrified
At the idea of regicide —
But still, he'd rather Duncan died
Than face Lady Macbeth! [II, ii]

Now to the famous Murder Scene.
'I wondered where on earth you'd been!
Some soap and water and we're clean!' [II, ii, 66]
Observes Lady Macbeth.

The Porter opens up the gate; [II, iii]
They find why Duncan's slept so late,
And things are in a fine old state
This morning, *chez* Macbeth!

Malcolm and Donalbain, the heirs,
Clear off to ponder their affairs;
So lawful precedent declares
The crown goes to Macbeth!

But all the time, he can't forget
That Banquo is a major threat.
The Witches said *he* would beget
More kings, and not Macbeth!

Two Murderers (or is it three?)
Treat Banquo with finality, [III, i]
Although his son escapes scot-free, [III. iii]
Which irritates Macbeth.

To celebrate their brilliant coup
The royals have a slap-up do —
And Banquo's there in spirit too,
Which disconcerts Macbeth! [III, iv]

By now he has a sneaking fear
That he is in it up to here;
And soon the Witches reappear
(This scene's been done to death) . . . [IV, i]

After the gastronomic Three
Have itemized their recipe
They cook a kind of fricassee
That ought to tempt Macbeth . . .

'Fear none of woman born; take care
If you should meet Macduff; beware
If Birnham Wood's no longer where
It's always been, Macbeth!'

Equivocation starts to bite . . .
'Is this a trick? Am I all right?
I'll murder everyone in sight,
In case!' resolves Macbeth.

At Edward the Confessor's court [IV, iii]
Macduff and Malcolm seek support:
Macduff is thrown by a report
That devilish Macbeth

Killed all his children and his wife
Whom he had left behind in Fife. [IV, ii]
'I've only got one aim in life —
To overthrow Macbeth!'

The Queen, observed by her physician, [V, i]
Somnambulates towards Perdition,
Washing her hands in
rapt contrition
For causing Duncan's
death!

In Birnham Wood, Prince
Malcolm's side [V, iv]
Cut branches from the trees,
to hide
Their numbers — and a
verdant tide
Encroaches on
Macbeth. [V, v]

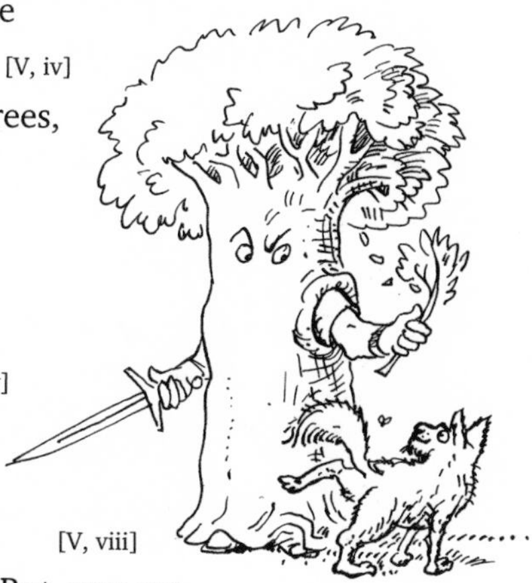

He meets Macduff.
'You can't hurt me! [V, viii]
You're born of woman!' 'But, you see,
I was delivered surgically —
Like Caesar was, Macbeth!'

Equivocation's had its way:
He's thrown eternal life away,
And nobody will ever pray
To reinstate Macbeth!

Enter Macduff, with Macbeth's head. [V, ix]
Malcolm will rightly rule instead;
But it could reasonably be said
That Fate destroyed Macbeth . . .

Measure For Measure

Measure for Measure's very dense:
You have to sift and weigh
The reasons deep and thoughts intense
That drive this 'problem play'.

The application of the Law
Is Shakespeare's interest here:
Should it be 'understanding', or
Inflexibly severe?

One issue's very up-to-date . . .
Right from the start we see
Top-down attempts to regulate
Public morality!

Vienna's worried Duke confides
That he must take the blame: [I, iii]
Statutes have slipped, and Virtue slides
Into the pit of shame,

So he has issued a decree
Which hands over the show
To his appointed Deputy —
Unbending Angelo.

The bawdy houses lose their trade,
And Mistress Overdone,
Pompey and suchlike folk, are made
Redundant in Act 1.

The Duke lets everyone surmise
He's upped and gone away;
But really, in a Friar's guise,
He's *primum mobile*!†

Now Juliet and Claudio,
Although not married yet,
Went further than they ought to go . . .
It's clear that Juliet

Accepted Claudio's embrace:
His act of procreation

---

† First Mover, or manipulator:
He reappears as Duke much later.

(With Angelo's regime in place)
Demands decapitation!

Poor Claudio, clapped in a cell,
Persuades a friend to see
If his chaste sister Isabel
Will soothe the Deputy . . . [I, ii]

She goes to Angelo, and pleads: [II, ii]
'Oh, let my brother live!
Weak men use power for their
needs —
Only the strong forgive!

'If he was in your Honour's place,
He'd let you off, I know . . .
Is your past free of all disgrace —
As clean as driven snow?'

His ice-cold blood is raging now,
Enkindled by her fire:
He's simply *got* to find out how
To work off his desire!

He makes a proposition: [II, iv]
'Claudio keeps his head

With absolute remission —
If you will share my bed.'

This comes as something of a
shock.
'I'm absolutely sure
My brother would prefer the
block —
And keep his sister pure!'

But Claudio, to her dismay,
Is less enthusiastic. [III, i]
'You ought to let him have his way —
It's utterly fantastic!'

'You beast!' she cries. 'How could you bear
To live on in my shame!
You mean to say that you don't care
About my virtuous name?'

Eavesdropping on her sharp rebuke,
The puller of the strings
(In other words, the secret Duke)
Begins arranging things . . .

A trap ensnares the Deputy,
Who thinks that Isabel [IV, i]
Waits in the dark — but he can't see,
And so he cannot tell

That Mariana, whom he swore
Contractually to wed,
And jilted several years before,
Is really in the bed![†]

---

† The fellow really should have twigged
The assignation had been rigged;
Since Mariana had to mumble,
You'd think an utter fool would tumble.

But Isabel's deceived as well . . .
She thinks that Angelo
Has axed her brother — so she'll tell
Her story, blow by blow!

Both ladies come to plead their case;
The Duke drops his disguise,
And Angelo's complete disgrace
Will come as no surprise!

In this enormous final scene [V, i]
A host of revelations
(Reminding us of *Cymbeline*)
Sort out some permutations . . .

The Deputy's estrangement
From his promised wife is healed,
And the lovers' long engagement
Is at last in marriage sealed.

And Isabella . . . did she guess
She'd be the Ducal choice?
She doesn't answer 'No' or 'Yes' —
Perhaps she's lost her voice!

The Merchant of Venice

Antonio would like to lend
Three thousand ducats to his friend [I, i]
Bassanio, who's in contention
For Portia, whom I'll later mention.
Antonio has an argosy
Of merchant ships: they're all at sea,
And till some vessels get to port
He's going to be rather short.†
However, being very fond
Of his young friend, he signs a bond
With grasping Shylock, whom he hates
Because of his excessive rates. [I, iii]
People in need prefer to go
To generous Antonio —
The charge on which his
    money's lent
(An APR of 0%)
Is causing Shylock some distress
Since it affects his business!
The fatal bargain's duly made . . .
The Merchant, if the bond's unpaid,

---

† *Antonio*. In sooth, I know not why I am so sad.
It wearies me; you say it wearies you: [I, i. 1]

Is by this reckless deal bound
To let the Jew remove a pound
Of flesh from somewhere on his breast —
To pay the loan, plus interest!

*

The lottery for Portia next: [I, ii; II, vii & ix]
Three caskets, each one
 with a text
Whose riddle (plus the
 kind of metal
The box is made of)
 ought to settle
Which enigmatic lock and key
Will open up her dowry!

Bassanio, to her delight
(And his, I may add) gets it right; [III, ii]
But hardly is the first glass drunk
When news arrives. Antonio's sunk —
At least his ships are, so it's said:
His wealth lies on the ocean bed,
And Shylock's sharpening his blade!
At this point, Portia tells her maid [III, iv]
They'll chase after Bassanio (who
Has gone to see what he can do)
In male dress. Of course, our eyes
Will penetrate their joint disguise

As learned Counsel and his Clerk —
Though all the rest are in the dark!

I'd be surprised if you don't know
How *Shylock v. Antonio* [IV, i]
Turns out. The bond to which they swore
Lets Shylock, by Venetian law,
Remove his pound of Christian meat;
The judge and witnesses entreat
In vain, and Portia's view is sought,
To guide the verdict of the Court.
She makes the Jew believe he's right,
And that his case is water-tight;
But just before his first incision
She tells him (with extreme precision)
That flesh itself is all his meed† —
To shed *blood* is a heinous deed

† A word the Bard has used elsewhere:
It stands for recompense, or share.

For which his goods are confiscate . . .
Moreover, if the measured weight
Differs from what it ought to be
(Albeit only fractionally) —
He's had it! But instead of showing
The Mercy he was charged
with owing,
The law now seems to
think it just
To crush the wretched man to dust.
Taking his goods should have sufficed:
To force his baptism in Christ
Is surely going a bit far . . .
A topic for a seminar?

*

Antonio's party are delighted,
And learned Counsel is invited
To state the necessary fee.
'No, no — my services are free . . .
But you, sir,' (to Bassanio)
'In view of what you feel you owe,
Might let me have your finger-ring.'
He'd rather give her anything
Than that, since he had told his wife
This ring's more precious than his life —
She gave it to him as a token
Of love that will remain unbroken! [III, ii]

Portia enjoys his consternation,
Stuck in this no-win situation:
Bassanio, hideously torn†
Between commitments, is forsworn
And takes the jewel from his hand . . .
So we can fully understand
The poor man's guilt when, later on,
His wife asks where the ring has gone! [V, i]
Well, this is just a bit of fun;
All is revealed to everyone,
And splendid news has just arrived —
Three of Antonio's ships survived
And reached port safely after all.
On this note, let the curtain fall!

† The same dilemma that we've seen
Face Posthumus in Cymbeline!

The Merry Wives of Windsor

'Good Master Shakespeare!' said the Queen:
'Jack† Falstaff is a treasure!
The wittiest stuff I've ever seen!
It is my royal pleasure
To see more written for this part . . .
Think of a merry plot
That shows him struck by Cupid's dart —
Two weeks is all you've got!'

† He's 'Jack' and 'John' at different times,
Which helps when sorting out the rhymes.

Whether or not this story's true,[†]
The Fat Knight was a hit
In *Henry IV* Parts 1 and 2 —
So why not build on it?
Falstaff's revival in this play
(With others whom we've met)
Advances them to Shakespeare's day,
Among the Windsor Set!

He mailshots Mistress Ford and Page
With flowery invention, [I, iii]
Well-calculated to engage
Their separate attention . . .
'You're past your heyday? That's all right —
We'll get on even better!
I'll be your Knight by day and night . . .
Reply by word or letter.' [II, i]

The Merry Wives to whom he's sent
This touching *billet-doux*
Compare his self-advertisement.
'He wrote the same to you!'
Cries Mistress Page to Mistress Ford:
'I've lost all trust in men!
If I let *that* weight come aboard
I'd never sail again!'

† John Dennis, an 'adaptor', who
Brought out in 1702
A modern version, is the source —
He could have made it up, of course!

They want to show him up; and so
They ponder stratagems,
And settle on a plan to throw
The fellow in the Thames.
To get him in their power,
Mistress Ford will be the bait:
'I can let you have an hour —
To be honest, I can't wait!' [II, ii]

Her husband, who is in some doubt
About her disposition,
Disguised as 'Brook' seeks Falstaff out,
And makes a proposition.
'You've met Ford's wife? I want to know
If she's a willing sort,
And just how far she cares to go . . .
I'll pay for your report!'

'Her knavish husband,' says Sir Jack,
'Is going out at ten.
I'll let you know when I get back
And we meet up again!'
By now, I'm fairly sure you'll say
You've sorted out the class
Or *genre* of this merry play —
Elizabethan farce!

The famous Laundry Basket scene [III, iii]
When Falstaff is immersed
In washing that is none too clean
Is what we think of first!
But misused words and verbal games
Play just as large a part
When three contestants lay their claims
To win Anne Page's heart . . .

A Frenchman, Caius — pronounced as Keys;
Slender — a bag of nerves;
And handsome Master Fenton — *he's*
The husband she deserves!
(In this one-off work of Shakespeare
The modern age is seen,
For the folk who entertain us here
Are subjects of the Queen.)

Beneath Herne's Oak, in Windsor Park, [V, v]
Falstaff is brought to bay;
And Anne, in the conniving dark,
Keeps well out of the way
Until the suitors she has spurned
Have married, by deceit,
Her copy; amity's
    returned —
And so our play's complete!

A Midsummer Night's Dream

1. The Spirits

Attention, you mortals — King Oberon speaking!
My Queen has adopted a boy, and I'm seeking
(By persuasion or threat) to get her to agree
To pass all her rights in him over to me. [II, i]
But wilful Titania keeps saying 'No!'
So I've utilized Puck, and told him to go
And fetch me a flower, whose essence I'll squeeze
On her eyes while she sleeps; and the next thing she sees
(I hope it's *revolting*) she'll love to distraction —
From which I'll derive some perverse satisfaction!

2. Puck

Puck is at my command, and obliged
to obey;
And he's keen to be useful . . . but if
there's a way
Of causing commotion, he will — so watch
out,
Helpless mortals, if you suspect Puck
is about!
He can take any form, whether live or inert,
And make sounds that will frighten, annoy or divert;
And he's *fast*: at the speed he returned with that flower
He'd go right round the planet in less than an hour!†

3. The lovers

Their trouble begins with the fateful decree
Of Hermia's father, who wants her to be
The wife of Demetrius, though she aspires
To marry Lysander (which he also desires). [I, i]

† *Puck*. I'll put a girdle round about the earth
In forty minutes. [II, i, 175]

Her bosom pal Helena, equally fair,
For Demetrius hungers, but *he* doesn't share
Her feelings at all — in fact, he can't stand her!
After Hermia's pondered it all with Lysander†
They decide to elope . . . they will meet up that night
In a wood, but Demetrius follows
their flight,
With Helena after him, hopelessly
calling . . .
With them all in the dark, the
confusion's appalling!
I'm there too, with the juice to apply to
my Queen;

[II, i]

And tell Puck to allay the confusion I've seen
By doping Demetrius, and ensuring he wakes
When Helen's in view! But since Puck mistakes
One young man for the other, disaster ensues,
For *Lysander's* the person whose eyes he imbues [II, ii]
With a yearning for her on whose face they alight;
And since Helen's the first to come into
his sight

† *Lysander*. The course of true love never did run smooth. [I, i, 134]

When he wakes from his doze, he's completely besotted
With the wrong girl, who's startled, and tells him:
'Get knotted!'
What I ought to have done was get Puck to
apply
Some restorative drops to his
misinformed eye;
But instead I compounded the
error by treating
Demetrius too. Now both men
are competing [III, ii]
For Helen — although she was sad on her own,
She now wishes these jokers would leave her alone!

4. The posh wedding
The plans of Duke Theseus, right at the start, [I, i]
To marry Hippolyta, don't form a part
Of the action again until quite near the end,
When he and his bride and the lovers attend
A play, or more aptly, a comedy show
Put on by the folk in the section below . . .

5. The players
Six artisans, led by a carpenter, Quince, [I, ii]
Have been learning their various parts ever since
The wedding was fixed, in the hope that their play
Will be the Duke's choice to be shown on The Day.

The most famous of all is Nick Bottom, a weaver,
On whose head, in rehearsal, my Puckish deceiver [III, i]
Claps the form of an ass, which Titania beholds
When she wakes. Her eyes dazzled, she gently enfolds
This thing to her bosom: 'What a beautiful head!
May I fondle your ears? Come into my bed!'

When I unglaze her eyes, as shortly I will,
Her paramour's face makes her feel quite ill: [IV, i, 77]
'How could I have loved such a horrible beast?'
So there should be a truce — for a short time, at least!

6. The course of true love . . .

Puck has squeezed a few drops of restorative stuff [III, ii]
On demented Lysander — they should be enough
To make him and his Hermia friendly again;

And though Helen must wonder what motivates men,
At least she has got her Demetrius hooked! [IV, i]
That very same day, the weddings are booked,
Since the Duke and Hippolyta, finding the four
In the wood, ask that Hermia's father withdraw
His ban on Lysander — so they're all happy now . . .
The couples are bound by their marital vow,
The actors are called, and down they all sit [V, i]
To embellish the drama with comment and wit.†
Then they go off to bed, and I wish them good luck;
But the last valediction is spoken by Puck:
If we shadows have offended,
Think but this, and all is mended,
That you have but slumbered here
While these visions did appear . . .

† *Hippolyta*. This is the silliest stuff that ever I heard. [V, i, 207]

Much Ado About Nothing

Question: Name the lovers who
Have leading roles in *Much Ado* . . .
Beatrice and Benedick?
That gets only half a tick!
Claudio's and Hero's pact
Matters just as much; in fact
Without their convoluted knot
There'd be no semblance of a plot.

*

Within Duke Leonato's mansion —
No, wait — that leads to awkward scansion . . .
Beneath Duke Leonato's ceiling
(Young, single, wealthy and appealing)
Both heroines are domiciled.
Hero is his only child,
But she's been brought up with his niece,
The extraverted Beatrice!
The burgeoning imbroglio
With Benedick and Claudio
Begins when they arrive to stay [I, i]
(They're officers who've been away

Serving in some campaign or other
With Don Pedro and John, his brother,
Who also turn up at the door
And plan to stop a month or more).
Beatrice, we quickly tell,
Knows Benedick extremely well
(To simplify the poetry
I'll henceforth call them B & B),
And arrows tipped with piercing wit
Fly to and fro, but do not hit —
Or rather, are returned in kind.
True love is, by tradition, blind
And silent — B & B, I sense,
Use repartee as a defence:

A kind of fear, a kind of pride,
Makes each their own emotions
hide.
Claudio is not like that:
Hero knocks the fellow flat,
But, being too abashed to ask,
Don Pedro does so in a mask [II, i]

On his behalf (which does not say
Much for his gumption, by the way).
Stuck by the touchline, looking on,
Is Pedro's bastard brother John —
An interesting mental case
Who's worthy of a higher place
Among the folk Shakespeare would use
To upset, harass or confuse.
Since Claudio's his *bête noire*
He comes up with a way to bar
The scheduled marriage which, to us,
Seems utterly ridiculous: [II, ii]
And since things go from bad to
worse,
I'd better start another verse.

*

Two scenes, amusingly absurd, [II, iii & III, i]
More than deserve a passing word,
When B & B, by shrewd connivance,
And unsuspecting of contrivance,
Are made to pick up hints revealing
The passion that the other's feeling —

It's excellent for the spectators
To watch such smooth manipulators![†]
So now for Don John's wicked scheme.
Hero's maid Margaret makes it seem
As if her mistress, and not she,
Leans from her window wantonly,
Conversing with a man below
(John's henchman, called Borachio),
Supposed no stranger in her life.
Claudio sees his would-be wife
(As he thinks) in these goings-on,
Having been prompted to
 by John;
And though no judgement
 could believe
That gentle Hero would deceive,
We let that pass and say 'Okay'
Because it is that kind of play.
But now a darker interlude
Constrains the optimistic mood . . .
The wedding's booked, the feast is spread,
Sweet Hero's to the altar led; [IV, i]
Then Claudio says she isn't chaste,
But loose, and utterly debased!

† More famous, but perhaps no better,
Is Act 2 Scene 5 of *Twelfth Night*:
We're waiting for the teasing letter
To come into Malvolio's sight.

Imagine Hero's consternation
At this amazing allegation —
And everybody else's too!
Not the most thoughtful thing to do!
'For this disgrace, my daughter dies!'
The shattered Leonato cries.
The bride's passed out, the wedding's wrecked
(You get the general effect);†

But then the Friar plays his part:
'We'll soften doubting Claudio's heart
By making out that Hero's dead;
He's obviously been misled,
And Time may bring the truth to light . . .'
The fellow's absolutely right!

*

† *Benedick*: This looks not like a nuptial. [IV, i, 68]

Enter the Watch — a comic lot
I've had to skip, because the plot
Has had to be elaborated;
But they are justly celebrated,
Especially Dogberry, their chief,
Who mangles words beyond belief. [V, i]
They overheard Borachio [III, iii]
And others who were in the know,
Planning the midnight assignation,
And seized them. At this explanation
Claudio bitterly repents
His unkind action, and laments
Before his lady's sepulchre
The dreadful thing he did to her . . .
And then, guess what? To make his peace,
He marries Leonato's 'niece',
In form not unlike Hero, who
Remains masked till he says 'I do' . . .
And B asks B if she (or he)
Will do the same — and both agree![†]

† *Benedick*. The world must be peopled. When I said I would die a bachelor, I did not think I should live till I were married. [II, iii, 233]

Othello, the Moor of Venice

I'm Ensign Iago, thought honest and true:
Three senators backed me, and said
That the job of Lieutenant was one I could do . . .
But *Cassio* got it instead!

I ask you! The guy's a complete amateur —
And he can't even drink (as we'll see)!
So I'm gutted to think that the Boss should prefer
This drawing-room soldier to me!

My Boss is Othello, a Moor. So what?
This is Venice, where many lands meet!
He's good at his job (making war), but he's not
Quite at home with the social élite!

Some incredible news reached my ears tonight — [I, i]
He's wooed, won and wed Desdemona,
So her father's gone off to challenge his right —
And to have her restored to her owner!

He complained to the Duke and the Council, in vain — [I, iii]
They're all worried about the position
Of Cyprus (which Turkey would like to regain),
And have given the Boss a commission

To set off at once: he's already aboard,
Torn away from the honeymoon bed.
So her father's submission was simply ignored . . .
'Make the best of it,' — that's what they said!

She's going as well. She's pursued, by the way,
By a stalker, a prat named Roderigo,
With more money than sense, who'll do just what I say,
As long as I flatter his ego.

So now it's Act Two, and our ships have arrived. [II, i]
The most up-to-date information
Says a storm wrecked the Turks,
and that no one survived —
So tonight there's a big celebration!

I've thought of a way to get Cassio's place . . .
Three bottles of wine at the most
And he's drunk — which on duty is such a disgrace
That I could be in line for his post!

What a night for a nuptial! It worked like a charm! [II, iii]
Roderigo, my gull, did the teasing:
There was such a commotion, they
rang the alarm —
Which the Boss found distinctly
displeasing!

So Cassio's had it — that's one-nil
to me!
Now then, can I build on success

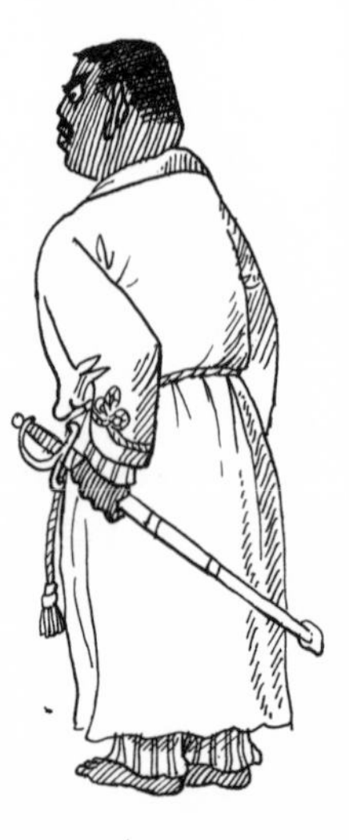

And discomfort the Moor? Yes, I
think I can see
How to cause him no end of distress . . .

I'll make Cassio ask Desdemona to
plead
With her lord to restore his position.
She'll do it, I know — which is all that
I'll need
To sow the first seed of Suspicion . . .

Then I'll work on the Moor, to make
him believe
Her affection is starting to stray.
Like all ladies (he'll think) she is prone to deceive,
And she's venturing Cassio's way!

I wish I could claim that the credit is mine,
That I'd plotted it all from the start . . .
For Scene 3 of Act 3 is, quite simply, *divine* — [III, iii]
Machination transmuted to Art!

I brought him to where Desdemona was seen
Giving Cassio friendly advice.
The embarrassed guy fled like some sly libertine;
And I muttered: 'That's not very nice!' [III, iii, 35]

Now I said it as though it was something I *thought*,
Not something I wished him to know;
And since Ensign Iago's a trustworthy sort,
I could tell he was thinking: 'Hallo . . .

That spontaneous utterance proves to my mind
He has already started to guess
That something is up; but because he is kind
It's the last thing he wants to confess!

Then — panic! By using her feminine skill
His wife got the Boss to agree
To have Cassio's case reconsidered; which will
(If he's pardoned) be curtains for me!

I had to regain the initiative fast.
The doubt I had put in his head
Would be hard to revive once the moment was past,
So I plucked up my courage, and said:

'Did Cassio know of your wooing?' 'He knew; [III, iii, 95]
And carried our messages. Why
Do you ask me? Does that sound suspicious to you?'
'No no,' I said (meaning Aye Aye!).

And I *knew* he was caught! I suggest that you read
The account in the relevant section:

Hints, prompts, innuendo; the use of 'Indeed!'
(Which needs the right sort of inflexion) . . .

Now my wife, Desdemona's companion, has found
What I think will confuse him still more —
Her mistress's handkerchief, dropped
on the ground!
It could be the ultimate straw . . .

I'll plant it on Cassio, then tell the
Moor
Where I saw it. If that doesn't bring
The required response, I could add that I'm sure
He was wiping his face with the thing!

What with that, and a cunning device that I used [IV, i]
To make him hear Cassio joking,
And assume that his wife was the lady abused —
His fire needs no further stoking!

Now he's made me Lieutenant (no more than I'm due),
And he wants to know Cassio's dead.
With regard to his wife, he accepted my view
That she ought to be strangled in bed.

I wasn't around when he 'put out the light' — [V, ii]
In other words, cut off her breath;

But I doubt if the wench put up much of a fight . . .
I should think she was frightened to death!

I asked Roderigo to wield the knife
And put Cassio out of the way;
But he botched it, and therefore I shortened
his life,
Since there's no knowing what he
might say! [V, i]

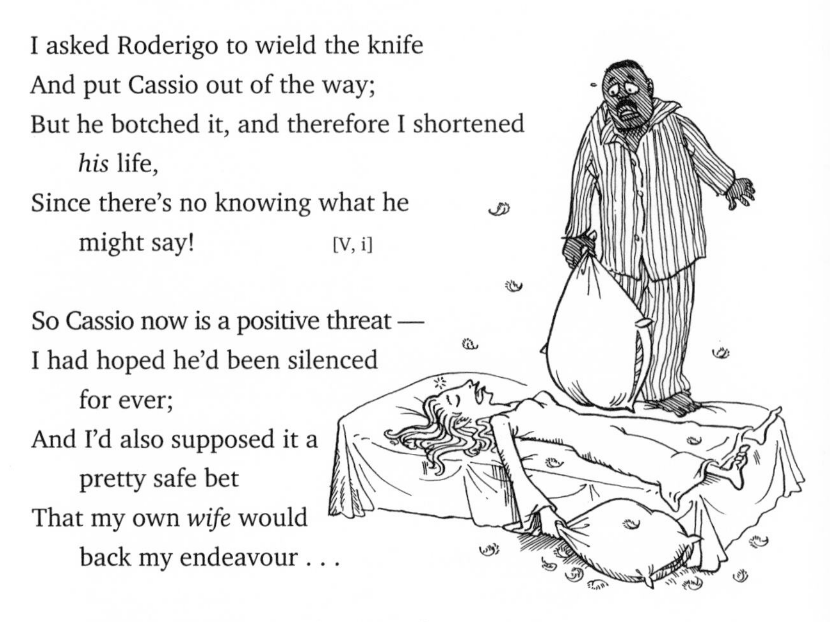

So Cassio now is a positive threat —
I had hoped he'd been silenced
for ever;
And I'd also supposed it a
pretty safe bet
That my own *wife* would
back my endeavour . . .

But seeing her mistress, she started to scream: [V, ii]
Told the Moor that I'd taken him in
With the handkerchief business — and blew the whole scheme!
So they've got me! I really begin

To wonder if Loyalty's somewhat *passé*?
I killed her, I have to admit . . .
The Boss had a few things he needed to say,
Stuck a knife in himself — and that's it!

Pericles, Prince of Tyre

Poor Pericles! I have to say
You're in a rather downbeat play.
It must have been a dreadful shock
To make that trip to Antioch
To win the princess, and discover
That her own father was her lover!
Your overwhelming tendency,
When going anywhere by sea,
To get wrecked on some alien shore
Is very awkward; furthermore,
Your wife dies as she bears Marina,
Who's fostered out . . . You've never seen her
Since that time: fourteen years have passed,
And here you are, standing aghast
Before her grave, reading her name
In chiselled stone; you're not to blame
If this sight sends you off your head
(Though neither one is *really* dead!).
But what must strike you extra hard
Is learning that the Stratford Bard

Wrote only 0.6 of you —
At least, that is the scholars' view;
And worse than all of this, to know
You're left out of the Folio![†]
Poor Pericles! I feel the need
To cheer you up — so let's proceed . . .

*

King Antiochus, as I've said,
Has claimed his daughter's maidenhead,

But unsuspecting suitors queue
To win her hand — our hero too.
Aspiring applicants must read
A challenging riddle to succeed,
But it's a no-win situation —
Failure decrees decapitation,
But since the answer gives away
The loathsome secret, come what may
They're for the chop! So Pericles
(Who solves it with the utmost ease),

---

† Published in 1623,
And cherished by posterity.

His life now hanging by a thread,
Clears off, and sails across the Med [I, iv]
To Tharsus (threatened with starvation)
With corn to feed the population.
This obviously goes down well,
And he remains there for a spell —
Cleon and Dionyza's guest,
Partaking of a well-earned rest.
But Antiochus learns he's there:
For safety's sake, he moves elsewhere . . .

*

Storm No. 1 casts him ashore [II, i]
At Pentapolis, just before
Another crowd of hopefuls meet
At King Simonides's seat
To have a fight, and then a dinner, [II, ii]
Before they're told the lucky winner
Of Princess Thaisa. Guess what?
Prince Pericles out-jousts
the lot!
She tells him: 'You're
the man for me,'
And we've already
reached Act 3.

*

It's at this point, most experts say,
That Shakespeare's hand informs the play.

King Antiochus has departed;
Thaisa's labour's almost started,
So they decide it's time to go
Back home; but Storm 2 starts to blow, [III, i]
And, tossed about upon the water,
His wife presents him with a daughter,
And dies (at least to outward eyes).
'I'm sorry, sir!' the seaman cries:
'A corpse on board's a well-known curse,
And only makes the weather worse —
She'll fit into this box all right,
And luckily it's water-tight!'
They throw Thaisa overboard:
Washed up, the lady is restored [III, ii]
By Cerimon, who, as we see,
Practises homoeopathy.
Pericles reaches Tharsus, where [III, iii]
He leaves Marina in the care
Of Cleon and of Dionyza,
Who will eventually despise her
(A desperate rhyme), since
this fair maid

Puts their own daughter in the shade.
But fourteen harvests are brought in
Before the fourth Act can begin . . .

*

Act 4, I'm sure you will agree,
Contains some splendid comedy.
Marina's secret death is planned
At Dionyza's servant's hand;
But just in time he's interrupted, [IV, i]
And pirates take her, uncorrupted,
To Mitylene, where she's bought
To stock a house of ill-resort. [IV, ii]
The maid's angelic virtue means

We see some very funny scenes . . . [IV, v & vi]
Meanwhile, Pericles believes
She's dead: before her grave he grieves,
And sorrowfully puts to sea [IV, Prologue]
(A hint of Tempest No. 3):

He will not shave or cut his hair
Till timely death ends his despair.†
Well, at the whim of wind and tide,
His ship of sorrow is espied
And brought to Mitylene's harbour.
They try to make him see a barber,
But he will neither smile nor speak,
Nor utter so much as a squeak.

[V, i]

A maiden who could charm a stone
To poetry by grace alone
(No prize for guessing!) is invited
To help out — and they're reunited . . .
A pity this scene's tucked away
In such an uncommercial play:
Its pathos matches that in *Lear*. [V, iii]
The happy ending's very near . . .
The Temple of Diana's where
They go to offer thanks; and there [V, ii]
The Priestess proves to be none other
Than Thaisa, Marina's mother!
The Lord of Mytilene, who
Marina gave a talking-to
When visiting the house of shame,
Now makes a much more worthy claim:
So wedding bells will fill the air —
And Pericles will cut his hair!

---

† In fact, he had already said
He'd let his hair unscissored grow
Until his baby girl was wed –
And that was fourteen years ago! [III, iii]

Romeo and Juliet

The *Sonnet* is the form I will select
To tell this story of extreme devotion:
Two young lives (not to mention others) wrecked
Because they couldn't handle their emotion.
Romeo thrives on Love's ecstatic pain —
The more it hurts, the more he is elated;
Fair Rosaline has put him off again,
Leaving the lad exquisitely frustrated! [I, i]
Now Fate takes him in hand: he goes off, masked,
To revels in the home of Capulet, [I, v]
Where Montagues (his name) are never asked;
And here the lad's knocked out
by Juliet . . .
Their gaze sinks deeper than
the sharpest blade,
Their lips touch, and the fatal
contract's made!

He's in her orchard; she comes into view, [II, ii]
Presumably about to go to bed:
'Why do you have to be a *Montague*?
Why couldn't you be Smith or Brown instead?' [II, ii, 33]

Well, everybody knows what happens then:
She titillates him from her balcony,
Going inside and coming back again!
So now we move directly to Scene 3,
When Romeo to Friar Lawrence
speeds [II, iii]
To fix their rites as soon as he
is able,
And finds him gathering what
look like weeds,
Whose essence (with directions
on the label)
This holy man distils, and people use
To mimic Death and wake up when they choose!†

I'm bothered by the enigmatic Nurse,
Who helps this ill-starred match to go ahead,
And (when we reach a slightly later verse)
Lets down the coiled rope to Juliet's bed!
She is a cheerful soul, but seems to me
Ambivalent, an agent of destruction:
It's quite incredible if she can't see
That this defiant act will cause disruption . . .
But anyway, she serves the lovers well,
And tells her charge that things have been arranged:
The two must meet at Friar Lawrence's cell
To have their vows officially exchanged.

---

† Juliet uses some, prepared from flowers
That lay her out for two and forty hours. [IV, i]

This may, the Friar thinks, help to unite
Their families — and in a way he's right!

His married status kept in secrecy,
Romeo waits for night and Consummation . . . [III, i]
But here is Tybalt, his worst enemy —
A Capulet of no great toleration.
'Draw, villain!' Tybalt cries, infuriated
By Romeo's gate-crashing in
Act 1;
But Romeo smiles, because
they're now related,
And fighting cousins simply
isn't done.
Mercutio, Romeo's friend,
thinks he's gone soft.
'I'll thrash this fellow if you
won't!' he cries,
Unable to endure being scoffed
By strutting Tybalt; but he's stabbed, and dies —
So Romeo slays Tybalt in contrition,
Which puts him in a difficult position . . .

Now trouble's brewing! Romeo's banishèd
(Pronounce the 'e') in all the hullabaloo,
And to the friendly Friar's cell he's fled — [III, iii]
The poor man's never had so much to do.

'Cheer up, my son. The Prince
has been forgiving.
Banishment's mercy!' 'Beyond Verona's
walls, [III, iii, 17]
If Juliet's within, life's not worth living.
Banishment's worse than death.' 'Oh —
utter nonsense!
Tonight enjoy with her; but, in disguise,
At break of day to Mantua depart,
Where you'll be well concealed from
vengeful eyes
Till Prince and parents have a change of heart!'
The rope ladder† the newlyweds unites . . .
It's fortunate he has a head for heights!

Romeo is awoken by a bird.
'*Lullula arborea* — time to go!' [III, v, 6]
'No, dearest, it's *Luscinia* you heard —
There's quite a difference, as you ought to know!'
'Now look,' says Romeo:
'I've got to flee
To Mantua right now,
while it's still dark,
Not argue about
Ornithology:
That *wasn't* a nightingale
— it was a lark!'

† The ladder's let down from the Balcony –
A climbing feat we're not allowed to see!

So off to exile from beloved Verona;
And Juliet is simply horrified
When told she's due to have a
second owner —
Count Paris is to take her as
his bride!
Her natural reaction is 'Oh, hell!'
So back again to Friar Lawrence's cell . . .

To fix the date, the Friar's had a visit [IV, i]
From Paris. The desperate girl begins to cry.
'It's not a very good beginning, is it?
Don't make me marry *him*! I'd rather die!' [IV, i, 50]
Her desperation moves the harassed Friar:
'Of this distillèd liquor (say the 'e')
I'll let you have the dose you will require
To seem to lie in death's extremity.

Take it the night before your wedding day:
You'll be interrèd in the ancient vault
Where all your lot go when they pass away.
Then, with your marriage cancelled by default,
We'll whisk you off to join your banished lord,
And you'll find somewhere nice to live abroad!'

Although it sounds a slightly risky scheme,
They go for it, for want of something better.
This part of the intrigue works like a dream . . . [IV, v]
But there's a problem, since the vital letter
The Friar writes to Romeo, to say
What's going on, does not reach his address;
So we can sympathize with his dismay
When her demise is bruited. What a mess! [V, i]
Life has no meaning without Juliet . . .
To her dark monument by night he'll fly
With the most potent poison he can get,
Embrace her for the final time — and die.
And so Confusion's masterpiece we'll see
Within the sepulchre — Act 5 Scene 3!

Paris comes first. His flowery tribute's scattered; [V, iii]
But Romeo, mistaking the intruder,
Kills him, and feels absolutely shattered
To find it is the nobleman who wooed her.

A kiss — some parting words — the poison
swallowed . . .
He falls across the body of his mate . . .
His death, of course, immediately followed
By Juliet's yawn and stretching, just too late!
She plants the happy dagger in her breast,
And dies a second death, immortalized;
The Friar's machinations are confessed;
The postal services are criticized;
Her statue will be ordered right away —
Presumably the families will pay?

The Taming of The Shrew

Two damsels engage us
(One mild, one outrageous)
In a boisterous play
That's more shocking today
Than when it was penned —
Just wait for the end!
This contrasting pair
Are destined to share
The family riches —
An expectancy which is
Encouraging offers
To get at the coffers
Of Signior Baptista!
The junior sister,
Bianca (whose hair
I assume to be fair)
Is much more attractive,
And wooers are active.
As soon as he sees her,
Lucentio of Pisa

Becomes a new suitor
Disguised as her tutor
(He exchanges his things
With his servant, which brings
A further dimension
To the comic intention).
But they've all got to wait
Till the older girl, Kate
(Who's impossibly curst)†
Has been married off first.
No one could begin
To court Katherine
Without getting a clout —
So marriage seems out;

† Short-tempered, reactive,
And most unattractive.

And this *impasse* is what
Determines the plot . . .
Act 1 Scene 2: Enter
Her future tormentor! [I, ii]
Petruchio, seeking
A marriage in keeping
With his income and status,
Resolves the hiatus
By agreeing to woo
This impossible shrew.
Well, *woo's* not the word
(Such a notion's absurd):
If he means to contain her
He must act as her *trainer*!

In Act 2 Scene 1
The groundwork's begun
By making it plain
That she'll struggle in vain. [II, i]

'Your father's agreed,
So let us proceed: [II, i, 260]
From now on, you're fated
To be do-mesti-Kated!'
Confusion, not Force,
Is his tactical course . . .
At her insults he smiles;
Is deaf to denials;
Tells his friends that her
squealing
Is a way of concealing
Her secret delight:
'It was love at first sight!'
It's not clear if Bianca
Has reason to thank her,
For it's time to consider
Who's the wealthiest bidder
For *her* fortune and face —
I haven't much space
(Since Kate is the theme)
For Lucentio's scheme . . .
But he'll win his Intended
Before the play's ended!
Petruchio's late
For his marriage to Kate — [III, ii]
Arrayed like a clown
(It is called dressing down),

He wallops the priest
And won't stay for the feast!
Kate's training proceeds
By refusing her needs
And thwarting her hopes
Till she gives up and mopes.† [IV, i & iii]
Once this has been done,
The battle's half-won;
And he starts, two scenes later,
To re-edu-Kate her, [IV, v]
Or rather, to train
Her recalcitrant brain
Not to argue or fight
When he's wrong and she's right,
But simply say 'Yes, dear!'
In the last scene, their guests hear [V, ii]
Kate's famous address:

---

† *Petruchio*: My falcon now is sharp and passing empty,
And till she stoop she must not be full-gorged,
For then she never looks upon her lure. [IV, i, 177]

How To Make A Success
Of Your Marriage: i.e.
Be submissive, like me! [V, ii, 137]
This speech, if played straight
May well alienate . . .
So should Katherine speak
With her tongue in her cheek?
Or make out it's all part
Of the feminine art
Of *pretending* to lose
In the way that you choose?
For, despite the play's name,
Kate will never be tame!

The Tempest

Time to go, Prospero!
Book now for the Final Show!
Easy, with your magic art
To change the barometric chart,
Induce some unpropitious weather, [I, i]
And bring a varied cast together —
Wrecked upon your Island's shore
As you had been, twelve years before . . .

*

Duke of Milan you used to be
(Though happiest in your library!)
Till your brother claimed your seat,
And with your overthrow complete,
Left you drifting on the sea
With your child (Miranda, 3).
Luckily, a kindly lord
Had stowed some useful things on board,
Including books — and I expect
You've read them all since being wrecked!
You let Miranda, now 15,
Learn all this in the second scene. [I, ii]
Her general knowledge is profound
(Your teaching's obviously sound):

She understands the moves of chess,
And ought to be a great success
At Trivial Pursuits; but she
Knows nothing of Humanity.
You are her measure of mankind —
That demi-beast you chanced to find
Already here, called Caliban,
Can hardly be considered Man!
Why do you now inform the girl
About her past? Why froth
and swirl
The isobars? Because you
know
The time has come for you
to go!

*

You've wrecked a princely gathering:
The scheming Neapolitan King,

Who backed your brother's midnight coup
(And *he* is in the vessel too);
The King's own brother, just as black . . .
And here's the lord who thought to pack
Your precious books — a real friend!
But no one meets a watery end,
Thanks to your spirit, Ariel,
Who does his work extremely well,
Since all the nobles reach dry land,
Including princely Ferdinand,

The King's heir. Teased by Ariel's song,
This wondering Prince is led along
Until he sets eyes on Miranda,
And, quite unable to withstand her,
Says: 'Wow!' Your daughter stares in awe:
'The third† man that I ever saw; [I, ii, 445]

---

† So Caliban's more man than beast —
Or so Miranda thinks, at least.
His status, rights, and subjugation
Have furnished many a dissertation.

The first that's ever turned me on.
Father, I want him!' Whereupon,
Though glad these young things seem to be
Of orthodox polarity,
To keep your daughter's jewel sound
You get him carting wood around. [III, i]

*

The King, convinced his son has died,
Is, naturally, mortified,
And settles down to take a nap
To help get over this mishap. [II, i]
His brother would of course succeed
If Ferdinand's dead . . . 'A simple deed,'
Advises your fraternal kin:
'Unsheath your blade, and do him in!'
Vain hope in this enchanted isle!
Alerted to their purpose vile
By paraphysical transmission,
You hastily arrange a mission
For sprightly Ariel, who makes
An uproar, and the King awakes . . .

His man Stephano's reached dry land, [II, ii]
So drunk that he can hardly stand —
He's fortified himself by drinking
The sherry cask that stopped him sinking.
He and the jester, Trinculo,
Decide upon your overthrow
Once Caliban's explained what's what
(They give the demi-beast a tot
Which stuns his uncorrupted head
And puts him in their power instead).
Each afternoon, as he knows well,
You have a snoozle in your cell.
That is the time to do the deed . . . [III, ii]
But obviously they won't succeed!

*

Inside your charmed laboratory,
Cut off on all sides by the sea,
These guinea-pigs of yours display
The faults they'd rather hide away.

Did you have visions of Reform,
Of changing their degraded Norm?
Of course you didn't, Prospero!
You're old and learned; and you know
That people born under a star
Can never be but what they are.†
They're brought together, to confess . . . [V, i]
Miranda stops her game of chess
With Ferdinand (whom she's accused
Of cheating) and, somewhat confused,
Utters those words so often quoted:
'Oh brave new world. . .' But all
she's noted [V, i, 183]
Is what these scoundrels wear, to hide
The ignobility inside —
You underline the irony
By saying: 'It is new *to thee*.'
Well, that's the last act of the Show:
You break your staff, let Ariel go,
And sail homeward in their boat
(Miraculously still afloat),
Restored as Duke to all your lands,
Leaving the island in the hands
Of Caliban, whom you once taught
To think, and then to speak his thought . . .
And who, it's fairly safe to claim,
Was happiest before you came!

† Though now there is a tendency
To challenge this philosophy.

Timon of Athens

Oh Timon! How could you have been so
naïve?
For a man of your standing, it's hard to
believe
That you didn't see through all the self-
styled friends
Who abandon you once your
benevolence ends!

You lend on request, and it's interest-free;
People's gifts you repay by a factor of three;
You stand bail if anyone lands in a spot —
And only your Steward knows how much you've got!

Among the well-wishers who flock to your hall [I, i & ii]
Is curt Apemantus, who sees through them all.
'They're eating *you*, Timon!' he jeers,
as they feast — [I, ii, 39]
But you let him rant on, and don't
mind in the least.

I must also allude to the soldier of fame
Alcibiades, who will both flatter your name
And censure your enemies, after you're dead;
And ensure your contemptuous epitaph's read!

Your story is hardly the best of his plays,
Though it dates from that late and magnificent phase
When he'd finished *Macbeth*, and quite possibly *Lear* . . .
And a taste of the latter is evident here!

Ingratitude's central to both. You're dismayed
When you see how completely your friends have betrayed
Your driving belief (as suggested above)
That men are united by brotherly love.

The foreseeable crisis occurs in Act 2.
Some debts that you're owing are long overdue . . .
'Don't worry — I'll call on my friends. I've no doubt
They'll be eager to help, and will bail me out!' [II, ii]

Well, who would have thought it? They don't want to know,
Now the prodigal coffers are suddenly low! [III, i-iii]
As the bleak Apemantus so shrewdly foresaw:
'When the sun starts to set, people fasten the door.' [I, ii, 141]

You invite the whole lot to the ultimate meal, [III, vi]
Whisk the lids off the dishes, and thereby reveal
That there's nothing but water to drink (or to eat) —
So you drench all the diners, and beat a retreat.

You take to the woods; and, while digging for roots, [IV, iii]
You find gold, for whose gleam you now don't care two hoots.
So your friends reappear: 'How are you getting on?'
'I know what *you* want! Help yourselves! Now be gone!'

Some robbers attack you. Their vice they confess;
And, compared with the devious thieves who profess

To like you for yourself, they are far more appealing . . .
So you give them some gold, and say 'Carry on stealing!'†

It is now that the play becomes less than 'dramatic'.
Its plot loses force, and it's epigrammatic:
This crisis of love has so poisoned your mind
That you just go on raving and cursing mankind!

But your servants disturb your emotional view,
Since unlike all the rest they've been honest and true;
It's a scene of great power and pain, when we see
Your kind Steward rejected, in spite of his plea. [IV, iii]

Alcibiades, who was a genuine friend,
Is banished from Athens, which, right at the end,
Offers terms when they see that his army's arrived
(His part in the story's a little contrived) . . . [V, iv]

---

† *Timon*. Nothing you can steal,
But thieves do lose it. [IV, iii, 450]

By this time you are dead, and your epitaph's found
(But how did you bury yourself in the ground?).
Alcibiades speaks of the way you were slighted,
And he reads your own words, in which all are indicted:

Here Timon lies, who everyone distrusted. [V, iv, 69]
Read and pass by: you make me feel disgusted!

But I'm sorry, old friend, for I have to admit
You're not *quite* big enough to be counted a hit . . .
The heroes of Tragedy have to be Great,
Or we're not going to feel disturbed by their fate!

Perhaps that's why Shakespeare decided to leave
Your play in abeyance, as experts believe?
But I have to confess to a fondness for you . . .
So I'm glad your play made the First Folio too!†

† If it hadn't, it would doubtless have been lost –
As would some sixteen others, to our cost!

Titus Andronicus

The doings in *Titus*
Can hardly delight us —
At least, that is what
    I'd have thought.
Throats are slit, hands
    are lopped;
Tongues are sliced, heads are chopped;
And ketchup's consumed by the quart.

The venue is Rome.
Weary Titus comes home, [I, i]
With the Goths' Queen Tamora in chains,
Plus her children from hell.
He's lost one son as well,
But though grieving, he
    never complains . . .

He must have had plenty,
Since he's now buried twenty,
And has four left, despite all the slaughter.
Three more will die too . . .
Plus Lavinia, who
Has a hell of time as his daughter!

His martial renown
Means the Emperor's crown
Could be his, if he had the ambition.
But he says he'll decline
And support Saturnine,
Who, as heir, ought to hold Top Position.

Our hero's enraged.
Saturnine was engaged
To his daughter . . . but now they've untied
The Queen and her boys
(With much flourish and noise)
Tamora's the Emperor's bride!

Titus sliced up and grilled
Her first son; so she's thrilled
That Lavinia's innocent beauty
Is inflaming the others:
To assist these two brothers
Is a positive motherly duty!

Meet Aaron the Moor,
Her black paramour . . .
As Tamora's new baby confirms
(Or at least, by its tint
Gives a definite hint),
The two are on excellent terms! [IV, ii]

As a man of intrigue
Aaron's in his own league.
Two of Titus's offspring are framed;
And their sister's a sight —
She can't whisper or write,
So her ravishers cannot be named. [II, iii]

This scene is exacting
And tough on the acting —
It's the crux of this barbarous play . . .
Hands chopped at the wrist;
Her tongue sorely missed —
It's a difficult part to portray!

But her father's distress
At the general mess [III, i]
Is convincingly shown, by revealing
His frenzied belief
That his only relief
Is to suffer the torture she's feeling . . .

More scope for disaster,
Of which Aaron's a master!
'Your two sons will come to no harm [III, i, 151]
If you lend me an axe
To take a few whacks
At the thing at the end of your arm!'

'A good friend indeed!
It's just what I need!'
So more ketchup to garnish the scene . . .
But now his hand's gone,
Titus muses upon
How exceedingly useful it's been!

And now what? His fist
Plus two heads that he'd kissed
Are presented to him on a tray.

And his last son is banned — †
So we quite understand
If his reason begins to give way . . .

Lavinia looks
For some stories in books
Like her own, which they half-understand . . . [IV, i]
So they give her a stick
And teach her the trick
Of tracing her tale in the sand!

Now the Goths have begun,
Under Titus's son,
To prepare for a massive attack.
Tamora tells Titus:
'Tell him *please* not to fight us —
I promise he'll be allowed back!' [V, ii, 112]

He replies: 'I will need
My son's life guaranteed;
So leave your boys here. Off you go!'
They are hung up like goats,
He cuts both their throats,
And Lavinia catches the flow.

† He slaughtered a son
(Who did not show respect)
Back in Act 1 Scene 1
So the maths are correct!

And now for a scene [V, iii]
With a novel cuisine
That our hero is dying to try.
The lads are minced up,
And they all come to sup
On Titus's freshly-baked pie . . .

No one stays for the sweet
Once they learn that the meat
Is part of some people they knew.
Though Tamora's perturbed,
She is still more disturbed
When the chef, with his knife, runs her through.

It' s the very same blade
With which he's just made
A saint of his victimized child . . .
Saturnine, somewhat vexed,
Kills the chef; but *he's* next,
And everything gets a bit wild . . .

Well, I warned you the story
Is a little bit gory —
Which was evident as we proceeded.
Now Rome will be run
By Titus's son . . .
And we hope no more ketchup is needed!

Troilus and Cressida

In umbra Homeri vagor†

Prologue

Troy, the city of Priam, father of fifty sons,
Paris among them, and Hector, and Troilus hímself;
for seven years Troy has survived the siege of tented Greeks;
swiftly they had crossed the wine-dark sea to bring back Helen —
Helen, wife of Menelaus, brother of Agamemnon their king,
to seize her back from Paris, who stole her away.
This lady is the theme. Now we begin the play!

Act 1

Calchas, father of Cressida, fled from Troy to the Greeks;
left Cressida with Uncle Pandarus — a debauched fellow;
Troilus sighs for her ('Oh Pandarus, I'm crazy about her; [I, i]
when can I see her? — let me see her!');
Cressida is gone on him too, but doesn't
show it,
except to us in a soliloquy ('I mustn't seem
too keen!'). [I, ii]
Now we move to the next scene . . .

† 'I wander in the shadow of Homer.'

Agamemnon and the Greeks discuss what to do next, [I, iii]
Ulysses delivering his famous speech on Order and Degree:
order is upset because their champion Achilles is sulking,
dallying in his tent with his friend Patroclus,
and his foul-mouthed fool, Thersites, insults all and sundry;
now comes a challenge from Hector the Trojan . . .
'Greeks, I will meet your champion before the city walls —
name him!' (secretly hoping to bring out Achilles);
but to teach Achilles a lesson the Greeks nominate Ajax,
a thug, a man of no quality; and Achilles is offended.
Which is what they intended!

Act 2

We hear a lot of unpleasantness from Thersites, which I skip;
There is a Trojan policy review by King Priam and his sons, [II, ii]

who discuss whether they ought to return Helen
to the Greeks —
whether she is really worth all this kerfuffle . . .
there is a lot of close argument, it is the kernel
of the play,
Hector saying she isn't worth it, Troilus saying
she is;
he is an optimist about the human condition,
and I quote:
'She is a theme of honour and renown,
a spur to valiant and magnanimous deeds.'
But is she? Anyway, the Trojan
War proceeds . . .

Act 3

Cressida, a half-tamed bird, is brought fluttering to Troilus;
her Uncle Pandarus witnesses their vows,
Troilus saying: [III, ii]

'I will be the measure of all
future lovers:
'As true as Troilus's shall be their motto;'
Cressida replying in similar vein:
'If I am false (which I shan't
be of course)
Hold my name up as the
exemplar of duplicity.'
Well, we shall see!

Achilles, furious that he has not been chosen to meet Hector,
messages his rival to meet him after the match [III, iii]
for a jar or two, a not unknown courtesy of the siege:
it has now gone on for so long that everyone knows everyone,
there are days off — it's nine-to-five warring,
And increasingly boring!

Act 4

The morning of the great combat starts badly,
for our lovers learn that Cressida's father Calchas
(you remember that he went over to the Greeks?)
has asked for her to be exchanged for a prisoner, [IV, ii]
so she's taken as an object of barter by the Greek
 Diomedes, [IV, iv]
who is a little too handsome for Troilus's peace of mind:
the Greeks kiss this attractive girl most familiarly
(she might perhaps have resisted more than she did) . . . [IV, v]

now for the combat between Hector and Ajax,
    a friendly joust,
rival fans mingling; in fact they don't fight very long,
and it's a draw anyway; post-match conviviality,
    no weapons;
Achilles and Hector meet (they have not, in fact, ever met
    before);
and Achilles offends the conventions by insulting Hector,
indicating the places where he will wound him when
    they meet for real . . .
This is not how heroes should behave, we feel.

Act 5

Troilus naturally seizes the chance of seeking out
    Cressida; [V, ii]
sees her being wooed by the Greek Diomedes — a
    mere hesitation
before she gives this man Troilus's love token;
Troilus's universe is shattered . . .

now the boast of Achilles is answered, Hector is arming, [V, iii]
here he is bursting from the walls of Troy,
here is Achilles striding from his tent to meet him; [V, v]
now the squalid end of Hector, tamer of horses,
taken by surprise by Achilles' hitmen when unarmed, [V, viii]
the sun setting, his body dragged in triumph,
the Greeks ascendant, Troy's walls about to fall,
And Troilus screaming vengeance. That is all. [V, x]

This mordant and cynical play
Is acted more often today
Than ever before;
It is rough-edged and raw,
So I thought I would write it this way!

Twelfth Night, or, What You Will

Is *Twelfth Night* the most perfect play
That Shakespeare would complete?
If pressed to name one, I would say
That nowhere else did he display
The same ability to weigh
The bitter and the sweet!

It dates from the creative height
Of *Hamlet* and *King Lear*.
His touch is absolutely right,
The comedy is sheer delight,
The passion stretched, but not too tight —
As shortly will appear . . .

Twins so alike, you might suppose
The sister was the brother.
They're on a voyage; a tempest
    blows;
The vessel to the bottom goes;
But they survive, though neither knows
What happened to the other. [I, ii]

When Viola, to her surprise,
Is safely cast ashore,
She finds a post (in male disguise) [I, iv]
At Count Orsino's court, and sighs
For his embrace; but he just eyes
Olivia, next door . . . † [I, i]

Who is an interesting case!
Her brother's died; and so
She favours black, and veils her face,
And plans to mope about the place
Till seven years her grief efface.
'Now then, Cesario . . .' [I, iv, 15]

(The Count uses the soubriquet
That Viola goes by)
'Visit this maid without delay,
And plead my suit in your own way;
Your youth may urge what I can't say —
At least it's worth a try!'

Our heroine must acquiesce,
And utters, from the heart, [I, v]
The words she's longing to express
About the love she can't profess
For him for whom she woos — unless
She steps out of her part . . .

---

† *Orsino*. If music be the food of love, play on,
Give me excess of it, that, surfeiting,
The appetite may sicken and so die. [I, i, 1]

Olivia, despite her veil,
Now finds she's not immune.
The words of this entrancing male
Her vow of continence assail;
Her resolution starts to fail —
She tells him: 'Come back soon!'

But once the youth has gone away
She quickly calls her Steward.
'Malvolio, catch that fellow — say [I, v, 304]
He left this ring. Now don't delay!'
So Viola learns, to her dismay,
The lady's heart is skewered!†

Olivia keeps a Fool, to speak
The Truth; a maid-in-waiting;
There's Uncle Toby, whose physique
Contrasts with Andrew Aguecheek . . .
Malvolio finds their merry clique
Extremely irritating. [II, iii]

---

† *Viola*. Poor lady, she were better love a dream.
Disguise, I see thou art a wickedness,
Wherein the pregnant enemy doe much. [II, ii, 25]

To bring him down a rung or two,
They draw to his attention
Olivia's forged *billet-doux* [II, v]
Which ends: 'Prove that you love me too . . .
Cross-gartered stockings, dear, will do
To show me your intention!'

He greets his mistress in the style
Suggested in the letter.
'Malvolio, why do you smile? [III, iv]
That rig-up's absolutely vile!
Put him in darkness for a while,
Until he's feeling better!'

Now misconception's at its
    height,
For Viola's twin is here!
Bemused Sebastian has to fight
A duel, at which amazing
    sight [IV, i]
Olivia cries: 'Are you all right,
Cesario, my dear?'

'*Cesario*? By what strange spell [IV, i, 59]
Have I this lady won?'
The pair get on extremely well:
In less time than it takes to tell
They've booked the church and
    rung the bell
And Two are joined as One!

Logistical manipulation,
Which keeps the twins apart,
Increases our anticipation
Of the climactic confrontation . . . [V, i]
And after general consternation
The explanations start!

Once everyone knows who is who,
Viola gets her man;

Orsino finds he loves her too
(There's not much else that he could do) —
The wedding will be hurried through
As quickly as it can!

But there is ambiguity.
As others may remark.
Abused Malvolio, set free,
Declares undying enmity:†
Wherever there is Comedy
One person's in the dark . . .

Feste, the Fool, will improvise
Sharp comments on the way:
Dishonesty goes in disguise;
Fair words are good for truth and lies;
But this should come as no surprise —
For the rain it raineth every day! [V, i, 388]

† *Malvolio*. I'll be revenged on the whole pack of you.
Exit. [V, 1, 377]

The Two Gentlemen of Verona

Two young men, one of them in love,
Have in all things been hand-in-glove
(That couplet is extremely poor —
Love's hard to rhyme, unlike *amour*):
The hearts that Cupid thinks he'll stab
For this emotional kebab
Are Julia's and Proteus's.
The dreamy votary discusses [I, i]
His rapture with his lifelong friend;
But Valentine cannot pretend
To see the point — he's more inclined
To use his time to stretch his mind

Than wallow in disabling passion!
For such as he, it is the fashion
To sever one's provincial roots
And seek Milan's refined pursuits;
But here the fellow is waylaid
By Silvia, a feisty maid. [II, i]
She loves him too, though her position
(Child of the Duke) means competition
From the official nominee — [II, iv]
An absolute nonentity
Called Thurio. Meanwhile, there's been
A brief but quite affecting scene [II, ii]
When Proteus (who's told to go
To Milan too) says Cheerio
To Julia. Each gives a token
(A hint that one vow will be broken!) . . .

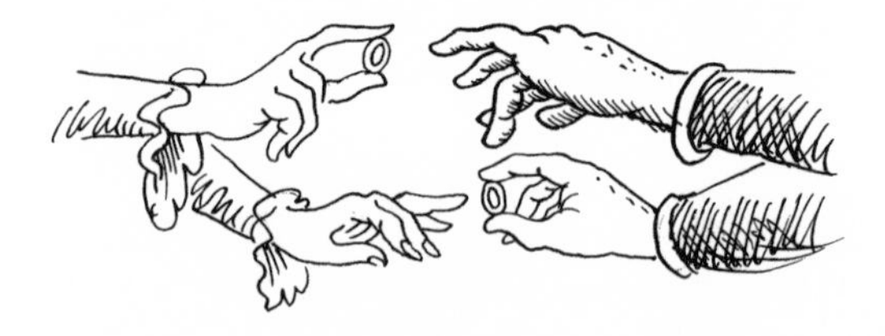

The moment Proteus sets eyes
On Silvia, his passion dies
For Julia, whom two scenes before
He said he'd love for evermore! [II, iv]

*

Such waywardness appears to us
Unpleasantly duplicitous;
But we're invited to suppose
The heart no moderation knows.
To use an image from the play, [I, i, 47]
Love, like a canker, eats away
His reason: thus, to gain his end,
Proteus now betrays his friend
(Who had, in all good faith, confided
That he and Silvia had decided
To do a bunk). The Duke's alerted,
The planned elopement is averted, [III, i]
And Valentine must lose his head
Or (sound the 'e') be banishèd.
The first choice doesn't seem too good,
So he is wandering in a wood
When, in a scene that strains belief,
Some outlaws take him on as chief . . . [IV, i]

But what is going through the mind
Of Julia, who stayed behind
When Proteus left? She pines and sighs, [II, vii]
And finally, in male disguise,
Sets off to join him, come what may.
Arrived, she hears a plaintive lay [IV, ii]
Twanged, bowed and sung beneath
the casement
Belonging to her own replacement —
'Who is Silvia, what is she?'
(You must know Schubert's melody).
Sleepy Silvia leans out:
'What's this dreadful noise about?
Proteus? What are you doing?
It's Julia you should be wooing!
Shoo — I want to get some kip!'
End of their relationship?
No way! Julia gets a job [IV, iv]
Working for this rotten slob —
She still pretends she is a man,
And calls herself *Sebastian*!
Enter a Dog, whom we first see
In Act 2 (when he steals Scene 3,
Showing us his frank opinion
Of Launce, who's Proteus's minion).
Launce is told to go and get
For Silvia, a canine pet:

It must be small, well-bred and yappy,
So Proteus is most unhappy
When told this mongrel thing was sent
As earnest of his sentiment
(*And* used the lady as a post).
But Julia is hurt the most . . .
Proteus tells her: 'Give this token
To Silvia, of whom I've spoken' —
The ring she pledged him in Verona
Is heading for another owner![†]
But, urged to marry Thurio,
Silvia now decides to go
And follow in her lover's track . . .
With Father *et al.* at her back. [V, ii]

*

† But Silvia is not deceived.
'I won't accept this ring.
It is the token he received
From Julia, poor thing!'

There isn't much I need to say
About the ending of the play —
No great surprises in this plot!
The forest outlaws catch the lot [V, iv]
(The Duke as well), but set them free,
And in the general clemency
These ruffians are reinstated.
Proteus is at last checkmated —
His quite astonishing retraction
Gives everybody satisfaction:
Both pairs of lovers are united,
And troths are generally plighted.
So that's the end of all the fuss —
Though I still don't trust Proteus!

The Winter's Tale

Exit, pursued by a bear. [III, iii]
Such dramatic directions are rare;
But like others I've met
(*Enter Pericles, wet*) [*Pericles* II, i]
They are tit-bits I'm eager to share!

Most people, I'm tempted to say,
Know the joke without knowing the play.
It is one I admire
(To put it no higher),
But it's not seen that often today.

Leontes, Sicilia's King,
Is convinced that his Queen had a fling [I, ii]
With Polixenes, when
She got pregnant again —
But Hermione did no such thing!

His jealousy comes in a flash.
He sees them together and —
Crash! [I, ii, 87]

Camillo, his aide,
Is told to put paid
To Polixenes: 'Give him
a dash

'Of some mortal infusion to drink.'
'Oh, very well, sir. If you think
It's what he deserves
I will steel my nerves,
And sort him out quick as a wink!' [I, ii, 345]

Now Camillo's a sensible guy . . .
Why should King Polixenes die?
So he throws in his lot,
Tells the dazed man the plot,
And they leave without saying goodbye! [I, ii]

This convinces Leontes it's true.
Hermione's baby is due,
So the lady is brought
Before the whole Court, [II, i]
With the proof of her crime in full view!

They all know this bizarre accusation
Is not based on the slightest foundation;
But he summons a lord:
'Take this bastard abroad,
And leave it to die of starvation!' [II, iii, 172]

We now jump to the episode where [III, iii]
The nobleman, chased by the Bear,
Must abandon it — maybe
This innocent baby
Will be brought up in
somebody's care?†

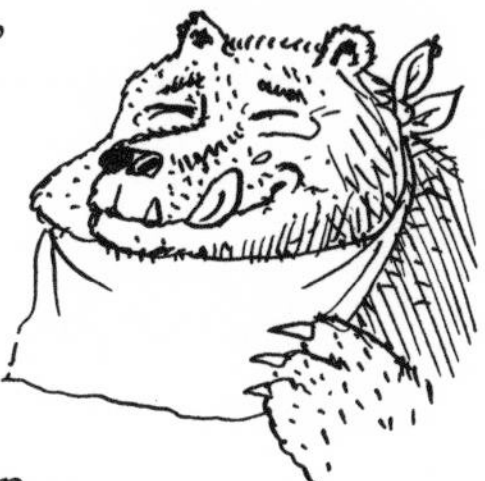

Meanwhile, to confirm his suspicion,
The King sends two men on a mission [II, i]
To Delphos, to see
What the verdict will be;
And they bring back Apollo's submission. . . [III, ii]

That the Queen has been true to his bed!
'This god must be clean off his head!' [III, ii, 140]

---

† *Lambs' Tales*, I think, are unfair to this lord,
When they say that his death was a rightful reward.
He wrapped it up well, and delivered a prayer. . .
So he didn't deserve to be scoffed by a bear.

Shouts Leontes, distraught;
Then a message is brought
That his son and his wife are both
dead!

Leontes is deeply affected.
It's now clear he should not have suspected
The Queen of deceit;
His despair is complete,
Both for them and the babe he rejected . . .

The baby's found, heaven be praised!
And by humble folk Perdita's raised. [IV, i (chorus)]
Now she's sixteen years old —
And lo and behold,
By her grace everyone is amazed!†

It's the time when the sheep must
be sheared
For their wool (which is why
they are reared);
And once the last
beast

† Noble birth will circumvent
The lowliest environment.

Has been fleeced, there's a feast —
For which all sorts of folk have appeared! [IV, iv]

In this scene of bucolic delight
(For most of the people are tight),
In the boisterous fun
Perdita is the one
Whom a Prince, Florizel, keeps in sight . . .

Here's his father, Polixenes, who
Has his visage well hidden from view!
He's heard of this maid
And is rather afraid
That his son has discovered her too . . .

Though Florizel's come in disguise,
He gets an unpleasant surprise
When the King says 'Ahoy!
Keep away from her, boy!' [IV, iv, 418]
And the maid, not surprisingly, cries.

But Camillo is there, and believes
That her outward appearance deceives . . .
This sweet shepherdess
Is Leontes' princess!
So with both of the lovers, he leaves

For the land that he left in disgrace [V, i]
(Though Florizel's father gives chase).
Leontes is thrilled
That the babe wasn't killed,
And everything falls into place . . .

Hermione's statue's on view. [V, iii]
It's simply too good to be true,
For in fact it's the Queen,
Whom no one has seen
Since the shambles in Act 3
Scene 2!

Leontes is utterly awed;
Paulina, the wife of the lord
Enjoyed by the Bear
Arranged the affair . . .
That's all 36 plays — please
applaud!

King Henry VIII & The Two Noble Kinsmen

How many plays did William Shakespeare write?
Three dozen I have now described to you
For which his claim is pretty watertight
(Apart from *Pericles*, Acts 1 and 2).
But there has been, and will be, much debate
About two other works I ought to mention . . .
Henry VIII was written very late
(After *The Tempest*) about the King's intention
To marry Anne Boleyn. Though we can tell
That much is written by another hand,
The Folio editors (Heminge and Condell)
Allowed his claim for authorship to stand.

Two Noble Kinsmen's first edition said
John Fletcher wrote it jointly with the Bard;
But, being published after they were dead,
Shakespeare's 'involvement' could be a façade
To gild its contents, and thus boost its sales,
For I can't see his genius in the writing!
It comes from Chaucer's *Canterbury Tales* — †
Two Theban warriors, great friends, end up fighting

---

† The *Knight's Tale* is the one it's based upon:
The friends are Arcite and Palamon.
The play appeared in 1634 –
Shakespeare reached heaven 18 years before.

To win a lady, sister of the bride
Of Theseus, with whom they are at war . . .
With this brief note you must be satisfied —
There simply isn't room for any more!